cool
food

cool food

MURDOCH
B O O K S

Contents

Starters

Beetroot hummus

80 ml (⅓ cup) olive oil
1 onion, chopped
450 g tin baby beetroot, drained
220 g (1 cup) ready-made hummus
2 garlic cloves, crushed
1 tablespoon ground cumin
1–2 tablespoons lemon juice

Heat 1 tablespoon oil in a frying pan, add the onion and cook for 3 minutes, or until soft but not brown.

Place the onion, beetroot, hummus, garlic, cumin and lemon juice in a food processor and process the mixture until it is smooth.

Transfer to a serving bowl, season with salt and pepper to taste and drizzle with the remaining olive oil.

Makes 3 cups

Cheese and chilli shapes

155 g (1¼ cups) plain flour
pinch dry hot mustard
90 g butter, roughly chopped
60 g (½ cup) grated vintage Cheddar
  cheese
4 red chillies, seeded and sliced
1 egg yolk

Process the flour, mustard and butter until they resemble fine breadcrumbs. Add the cheese and chilli, then the egg yolk and 1 tablespoon water, and process until the mixture comes together. Gather into a ball, cover with plastic wrap and refrigerate for 30 minutes.

Preheat the oven to 190°C (375°F/ Gas 5). On a lightly floured surface, roll out the dough to a 5 mm thickness. Cut into 5 cm rounds.

Place on lightly greased baking trays and bake for 15–20 minutes, or until golden. Cool.

Makes 26

Tzatziki

2 Lebanese cucumbers
400 g Greek-style plain yoghurt
4 garlic cloves, crushed
3 tablespoons finely chopped mint,
  plus extra to garnish
1 tablespoon lemon juice

Cut the cucumbers in half lengthways, scoop out the seeds and discard. Leave the skin on and coarsely grate the cucumber into a small colander. Sprinkle with salt and leave over a large bowl for 15 minutes to drain off any bitter juices.

Meanwhile, place the yoghurt, crushed garlic, mint and lemon juice in a bowl, and stir until well combined.

Rinse the cucumber under cold water then, taking small handfuls, squeeze out any excess moisture. Combine the grated cucumber with the yoghurt mixture then season to taste with salt and freshly ground black pepper. Serve immediately or refrigerate until ready to serve, garnished with the extra mint.

Makes 2 cups

Note: Tzatziki is often served as a dip with flatbread or Turkish pide but is also suitable to serve as a sauce to accompany seafood and meat. Tzatziki will keep in an airtight container in the refrigerator for 2–3 days.

Tahini and chilli palmiers

135 g (½ cup) tahini
1 red chilli, seeded and finely
  chopped
½ teaspoon paprika
2 sheets ready-rolled puff pastry,
  thawed

Preheat the oven to 200°C (400°F/ Gas 6). Combine the tahini, chilli and paprika. Spread half the mixture over each sheet of pastry (to the edges).

Fold the pastry from opposite sides until the folds meet in the middle. Then fold one side over the other to resemble a closed book. Refrigerate for 5 minutes to firm.

Cut into 1.5 cm slices and place on baking trays lined with baking paper (leaving room for spreading).

Bake for 8 minutes, then turn over and bake for 2 minutes, or until golden brown.

Makes 36

Cheese fruit log

35 g (¼ cup) shelled pistachio nuts
250 g cream cheese, softened
50 g (¼ cup) finely chopped dried
  apricots
3 spring onions, finely chopped
45 g (¼ cup) sun-dried tomatoes,
  drained, finely chopped
10 g (⅓ cup) finely chopped flat-leaf
  parsley

Preheat the oven to 200°C (400°F/ Gas 6). Place the pistachio nuts on a lined baking tray and roast for 5 minutes, or until golden brown. Cool and finely chop.

Beat the cream cheese until smooth. Fold in the apricot, onion and sun-dried tomato, and pepper to taste.

Form the mixture into a 20 cm log. Roll the log in the combined pistachio nuts and parsley. Wrap in plastic wrap and refrigerate until firm.

Makes a 20 cm log

Dolmades

275 g vine leaves in brine
185 ml (³/₄ cup) olive oil
2 onions, finely chopped
165 g (³/₄ cup) short-grain rice
6 spring onions, finely chopped
20 g (¹/₃ cup) chopped dill
1 tablespoon chopped mint
1 tablespoon lemon juice

lemon wedges

Rinse the vine leaves in cold water, soak in warm water for 1 hour and then drain.

Heat 125 ml (¹/₂ cup) of the oil in a large frying pan. Add the onion and cook over low heat for 5 minutes. Remove from the heat, cover and leave for 5 minutes. Add the rice, spring onion, herbs and lemon juice. Mix well and season.

Lay out a vine leaf, vein-side-up, on a plate. Place 3 teaspoons of filling onto the centre. Fold the sides over the mixture, then roll up towards the tip of the leaf. Repeat until you have made 42 dolmades.

Use five or six vine leaves to line the base of a large heavy-based pan. Pack the dolmades in the lined pan in two layers and drizzle with the remaining oil. Put a plate on top of the dolmades, to keep them in place, and cover with 375 ml (1¹/₂ cups) water. Bring to the boil, reduce the heat and simmer, covered, for 45 minutes. Remove the plate, lift out the dolmades with a slotted spoon. Serve either warm or cold with the lemon wedges.

Makes 42

Tapenade

400 g (2²/₃ cups) pitted Kalamata
  olives
2 garlic cloves, crushed
2 anchovy fillets in oil, drained
2 tablespoons capers in brine, rinsed
  and squeezed dry
2 teaspoons chopped fresh thyme
  leaves
2 teaspoons Dijon mustard
1 tablespoon lemon juice
60 ml (¹/₄ cup) olive oil
1 tablespoon brandy, optional

Place the kalamata olives, crushed garlic, anchovies, capers, chopped thyme, Dijon mustard, lemon juice, oil and brandy in a food processor and process until smooth. Season to taste with salt and freshly ground black pepper. Spoon into a clean, warm jar, cover with a layer of olive oil, seal and refrigerate for up to 1 week. Serve on bruschetta or with a meze plate.

Makes 1¹/₂ cups

Note: To make sure your storage jar is very clean, preheat the oven to very slow 120°C (250°F/Gas ¹/₂). Wash the jar and lid thoroughly in hot soapy water (or preferably in a dishwasher) and rinse well with hot water. Put the jar on a baking tray and place in the oven for 20 minutes, or until fully dry and you are ready to use it. Do not dry the jar or lid with a tea towel.

Prawn san choy bau

1 kg raw medium prawns, peeled and
   deveined, or 500 g raw prawn meat
1 tablespoon oil
1 teaspoon sesame oil
2 spring onions, finely chopped
2 garlic cloves, crushed
1 cm x 2 cm piece fresh ginger,
   peeled and grated
120 g drained water chestnuts,
   chopped
1 tablespoon chopped red chilli
185 g (1 cup) cooked white rice
90 g (1 cup) bean sprouts, trimmed
25 g (½ cup) chopped coriander
   leaves
2 tablespoons soy sauce
2 tablespoons oyster sauce
2 tablespoons lime juice
60 ml (¼ cup) hoisin sauce

Wash the lettuce and separate the
leaves. Shake off any excess water
and drain on paper towels.

If the prawns are large, cut them into
smaller pieces. Heat a wok over high
heat, add the oils, swirl to coat, then
add the spring onion, crushed garlic
and ginger. Cook for 30 seconds then
add the prawn meat, water chestnuts
and chilli, season with salt and
cracked black pepper, and continue
stir-frying for 2 minutes. Add the
cooked rice, sprouts and coriander
and stir until combined.

Add the soy sauce, oyster sauce and
lime juice, then remove from the heat.
Transfer the mixture to a serving bowl.
Place the dry lettuce cups on a plate
and spoon the prawn mixture into
each one. Serve with hoisin sauce.

Serves 4–6

Potato, olive oil and garlic dip

460 g (2 cups) mashed potato
3 garlic cloves, crushed
185 ml ($^3/_4$ cup) olive oil
2 tablespoons white wine vinegar
5 tablespoons milk
30 g ($^1/_2$ cup) chopped fresh herbs

Combine the potato and garlic in a bowl. Using electric beaters, gradually beat in half the oil, then the vinegar, then the remaining oil.

Slowly beat in the milk. Add the herbs and season to taste with salt and freshly ground black pepper.

Makes 21/2 cups

Linseed crackers

125 g (1 cup) plain flour
1/2 teaspoon baking powder
1/2 teaspoon sugar
2 tablespoons linseeds
60 ml (1/4 cup) milk
2 tablespoons olive oil

Preheat the oven to 200°C (400°F/ Gas 6). Process the flour, baking powder, sugar and 1/2 teaspoon salt. Add pepper to taste, and stir in the linseeds. Add the milk and oil and mix to form a wet crumbly mixture, adding extra milk if the mixture is too dry.

Turn the mixture out onto a flat, lightly floured surface and bring the mixture together into a ball.

Divide the mixture in half, place one half between two sheets of baking paper and roll out to a thickness of 2–3 mm. Prick liberally with a fork. Cut the dough into 12 irregular triangles and arrange in a single layer on a lightly greased baking tray. Repeat with the remaining dough.

Bake for 15–20 minutes, or until the bases are lightly golden. Turn over and bake for a further 4–5 minutes, or until the other side is also lightly golden. Transfer to a wire rack to cool completely.

Makes 24

Falafel

150 g (1 cup) dried split broad beans
  (see Note)
220 g (1 cup) dried chickpeas
1 onion, roughly chopped
6 garlic cloves, roughly chopped
2 teaspoons ground coriander
1 tablespoon ground cumin
15 g (½ cup) chopped flat-leaf parsley
¼ teaspoon chilli powder
½ teaspoon bicarbonate of soda
3 tablespoons chopped coriander
light oil, for deep-frying

Cover the broad beans with 750 ml (3 cups) water and leave to soak for 48 hours. (Drain the beans, rinse and cover with fresh water once or twice.) Place the chickpeas in a large bowl, cover with 750 ml (3 cups) water and soak for 12 hours.

Drain the beans and chickpeas and pat dry with paper towels. Process in a food processor with the onion and garlic until smooth.

Add the ground coriander, cumin, parsley, chilli powder, bicarbonate of soda and coriander. Season with salt and pepper, and mix until well combined. Transfer to a large bowl, knead and leave for 30 minutes.

Shape tablespoons of the mixture into balls, flatten slightly, place on a tray and leave for 20 minutes.

Fill a deep, heavy-based saucepan one-third full of oil and heat to 180°C (350°F), or until a cube of bread browns in 15 seconds. Cook the falafel in batches for 1–2 minutes, or until golden. Drain on paper towels. Serve with hummus, baba ghannouj and pitta bread.

Makes 30

Note: Split broad beans are available from specialist food stores.

Borek

400 g feta cheese
2 eggs, lightly beaten
25 g (¾ cup) chopped flat-leaf parsley
375 g filo pastry
80 ml (⅓ cup) olive oil

Preheat the oven to 180°C (350°F/ Gas 4). Lightly grease a baking tray. Crumble the feta into a large bowl using a fork or your fingers. Mix in the eggs and parsley and season with freshly ground black pepper.

Cover the filo pastry with a damp tea towel so it doesn't dry out. Remove one sheet at a time. Brushing each sheet lightly with olive oil, layer four sheets on top of one another. Cut the pastry into four 7 cm strips.

Place two rounded teaspoons of the feta mixture in one corner of each strip and fold diagonally, creating a triangle pillow. Place on the baking tray, seam-side-down, and brush with olive oil. Repeat with the remaining pastry and filling to make 24 parcels. Bake for 20 minutes, or until golden. Serve these as part of a meze plate.

Makes 24

Note: Fillings for borek are versatile and can be adapted to include your favourite cheeses such as haloumi, Gruyère, Cheddar or mozzarella.

Gravlax

1 teaspoon crushed black
  peppercorns
60 g (¼ cup) sugar
2 tablespoons coarse sea salt
2.5 kg salmon, filleted and boned
  but with the skin left on (ask your
  fishmonger to do this)
1 tablespoon vodka or brandy
4 tablespoons very finely chopped
  fresh dill

Mustard sauce
1½ tablespoons cider vinegar
1 teaspoon caster sugar
125 ml (½ cup) olive oil
2 teaspoons chopped fresh dill
2 tablespoons Dijon mustard

Combine the peppercorns, sugar and salt. Use tweezers to remove any bones from the salmon. Pat dry with paper towels and lay one fillet skin-side-down in a tray. Sprinkle with half the vodka, rub half the sugar mixture into the flesh, then sprinkle with half of the dill. Sprinkle the remaining vodka over the second fillet and rub the remaining sugar mixture into the flesh. Lay it flesh-side-down on top of the dill-coated salmon. Cover with plastic wrap and place a heavy board on top. Weigh the board downabnd refrigerate for 24 hours, turning the wrapped fillets over after 12 hours.

To make the mustard sauce, whisk together the vinegar, sugar, oil, dill and mustard, then cover until needed.

When the salmon is ready lift off the top fillet and lay both fillets on a board. Brush off the dill and any seasoning mixture with a stiff pastry brush. Sprinkle the fillets with the remaining dill, pressing it onto the salmon, then shake off any excess. Serve the salmon whole, on the serving board. Use a very sharp knife with a flexible blade to thinly slice the salmon on an angle towards the tail, and serve with the mustard sauce and dark rye bread.

Serves 20

Roast capsicum and eggplant spread

1 large (450 g) eggplant (aubergine), halved
2 teaspoons olive oil
1 red capsicum (pepper), halved
2 garlic cloves, crushed
15 g (¼ cup) chopped mint
3 teaspoons balsamic vinegar

Preheat the oven to 200°C (400°F/ Gas 6). Brush the cut side of the eggplant with some of the oil. Place cut-side-up on a baking tray. Brush the skin of the capsicum with the remaining oil and place skin-side-up on the baking tray next to the eggplant. Bake the eggplant and capsicum for about 30–35 minutes, or until the flesh is soft.

Place the capsicum in a plastic bag and leave to cool, then peel away the skin. Allow the eggplant to cool.

Scoop the flesh out of the eggplant and place in a food processor with the capsicum, garlic, mint and balsamic vinegar. Season to taste and process until smooth.

Makes 2 cups

Prawn pâté with garlic toasts

315 ml (1¼ cups) chicken stock
1 tablespoon gelatine
375 g cream cheese, at room
  temperature
800 g cooked prawns, peeled,
  deveined and roughly chopped
2 garlic cloves, crushed
2 tablespoons finely chopped chives
1 tablespoon chopped dill
30 g butter, melted
2 tablespoons olive oil
1 baguette, cut into 7 mm slices

Bring a shallow saucepan of water to the boil. Pour the stock into a heatproof bowl, then sprinkle the gelatine evenly over it; do not stir. Remove the saucepan from the heat and place the bowl of chicken stock in the pan. Stir the gelatine into the stock until it has dissolved; remove the bowl and cool for 30 minutes.

Place the gelatine liquid in a blender, add the cream cheese, half the prawn meat and half of the garlic and blend until smooth. Transfer to a bowl and leave for 20 minutes, or until thickened slightly.

Add the remaining prawn meat, chives and dill and season to taste. Pour into eight 125 ml (½ cup) ramekins. Cover with plastic wrap and refrigerate for 2 hours, or until set.

Preheat the oven to 180°C (350°F/ Gas 4). Combine the butter, oil and remaining garlic and lightly brush both sides of the bread slices with the mixture. Place apart on baking trays and bake for 10 minutes, or until golden and crisp. Leave to cool.

Unmould the pâté and serve with the garlic toasts.

Serves 8

Bruschetta

4 Roma (plum) tomatoes, chopped
80 ml (⅓ cup) olive oil
1 tablespoon balsamic vinegar
2 tablespoons chopped basil
8 slices day-old crusty Italian bread
1 garlic clove, peeled

chopped basil

Combine the tomatoes, olive oil, balsamic vinegar and chopped basil. Season well.

Toast the bread on one side. Rub the toasted side lightly with a peeled clove of garlic. Top with the tomato mixture and garnish with the extra chopped basil. Serve immediately.

Makes 8

Crunchy wedges

6 floury or all-purpose potatoes
1 tablespoon oil
25 g (1/4 cup) dry breadcrumbs
2 teaspoons chopped chives
1 teaspoon celery salt
1/4 teaspoon garlic powder
1/2 teaspoon chopped rosemary

Preheat the oven to 200°C (400°F/ Gas 6). Cut the potatoes into eight wedges each and toss in the oil.

Combine the breadcrumbs, chives, celery salt, garlic powder and rosemary in a bowl. Add the wedges and coat well. Place on greased baking trays and bake for 40 minutes, or until crisp and golden.

Makes 48

Chargrilled baby octopus

1 kg baby octopus
185 ml (¾ cup) red wine
2 tablespoons balsamic vinegar
2 tablespoons soy sauce
2 tablespoons hoisin sauce
1 garlic clove, crushed

Cut off the octopus heads, below the eyes, with a sharp knife. Discard the heads and guts. Push the beaks out with your index finger, remove and discard. Wash the octopus thoroughly under running water and drain on paper towels. If the octopus are very large, cut the tentacles into quarters.

Put the octopus in a large bowl. Stir together the wine, vinegar, soy sauce, hoisin sauce and garlic in a jug and pour over the octopus. Toss to coat, then cover and refrigerate for several hours, or overnight.

Heat a chargrill plate or barbecue hotplate until very hot and then lightly grease. Drain the octopus, reserving the marinade. Cook in batches for 3–5 minutes, or until the octopus flesh turns white. Brush the marinade over the octopus during cooking. Be careful not to overcook or the octopus will be tough. Serve warm or cold. Delicious with a green salad and lime wedges.

Serves 4

Chilled almond soup

1 loaf (200 g) day-old white Italian
  bread, crust removed
155 g (1 cup) whole blanched
  almonds
3–4 garlic cloves, chopped
125 ml (½ cup) extra virgin olive oil
80 ml (⅓ cup) sherry vinegar or white
  wine vinegar
315–375 ml (1¼–1½ cups) vegetable
  stock or water
2 tablespoons olive oil, extra
75 g day-old white Italian bread,
  extra, crust removed and cut into
  1 cm cubes
200 g small seedless green grapes

Soak the bread in cold water for
5 minutes, then squeeze to remove
any excess moisture. Place the
almonds and garlic in a food
processor and process until well
ground. Add the bread and process
to a smooth paste.

With the motor running, add the oil
in a slow steady stream until the
mixture is the consistency of thick
mayonnaise. Slowly add the sherry
vinegar and 315 ml (1¼ cups) of the
stock, or water, until the mixture has
reached the desired consistency.
Blend for 1 minute. Season with salt,
then refrigerate for at least 2 hours.
The soup thickens on refrigeration so
add more stock or water to reach the
desired consistency.

Heat the extra olive oil in a large frying
pan. Add the bread and toss over
medium heat for 2–3 minutes, or
until evenly golden brown. Drain on
crumpled paper towels. Serve the
soup very cold garnished with the
grapes and bread cubes.

Serves 4–6

Prawn, mango and macadamia salad

1 radicchio heart
25 g (½ cup) basil leaves, torn
30 g (1 cup) watercress sprigs
24 cooked king prawns, peeled
  and deveined with tails intact
3 tablespoons macadamia oil
3 tablespoons extra virgin olive oil
150 g (1 cup) macadamia nuts,
  coarsely chopped
2 garlic cloves, crushed
3 tablespoons lemon juice
1 ripe mango, cut into small dice

Remove the outer green leaves from the radicchio, leaving only the tender pink leaves. Tear any large leaves in half and arrange in a shallow serving bowl. Scatter with half of the basil leaves and the watercress, and toss lightly. Arrange the prawns over the salad leaves.

Heat the oils in a small, frying pan over medium heat. Add the nuts and cook for 5 minutes, or until golden. Add the garlic and cook for a further 30 seconds, then remove from the heat and add the lemon juice and mango. Season to taste, pour over the salad and scatter with the remaining basil leaves.

Serves 4–6

Pear and walnut salad with blue cheese dressing

Dressing
100 g creamy blue cheese
60 ml (¼ cup) olive oil
1 tablespoon walnut oil
1 tablespoon lemon juice
1 tablespoon cream
2 teaspoons finely chopped sage

100 g (1 cup) walnut halves
4 firm, ripe small pears, such as
  Corella
2 tablespoons lemon juice
2 witlof (chicory), trimmed and leaves
  separated
100 g Parmesan cheese, shaved

To make the dressing, purée the blue cheese in a small processor, then add the olive oil, walnut oil and lemon juice, and blend until smooth. With the motor running, slowly add 2 teaspoons warm water. Stir in the cream and sage, and season to taste.

Preheat the grill to medium–hot. Place the walnuts in a bowl and cover with boiling water. Allow to steep for 1 minute, then drain. Spread the walnuts on a baking tray and place under the grill for 3 minutes, or until lightly toasted. Chop coarsely.

Thinly slice across the pears through the core to make rounds. Do not peel or core the pears, but discard the seeds. As each pear is sliced, sprinkle with a little lemon juice to prevent discoloration. On each serving plate, arrange three pear slices in a circle. Top with a scattering of walnuts, a couple of endive leaves, a few more walnuts and some Parmesan. Repeat this layering, reserving the last layer of Parmesan and some of the walnuts. Spoon some dressing over each stack, scatter with the remaining walnuts, and top each with the reserved Parmesan. Serve as a first course, or as an accompaniment to simple meat dishes.

Serves 4

Prawns with saffron potatoes

16 raw medium prawns
80 ml (1/3 cup) olive oil
450 g new potatoes, cut in half
1/4 teaspoon saffron threads, crushed
1 garlic clove, crushed
1 bird's eye chilli, seeded and finely
  chopped
1 teaspoon grated lime zest
60 ml (1/4 cup) lime juice
200 g baby rocket

Preheat the oven to 180°C (350°F/ Gas 4). Peel and devein the prawns, leaving the tails intact.

Heat 2 tablespoons of the oil in a frying pan and brown the potatoes. Transfer to a roasting tin and toss gently with the saffron and some salt and black pepper. Bake for 25 minutes, or until tender.

Heat a chargrill pan over medium heat. Toss the prawns with the garlic, chilli, lime zest and 1 tablespoon of the oil in a small bowl. Grill the prawns for 2 minutes each side, or until pink and cooked.

In a small jar, shake the lime juice and the remaining oil. Season with salt and pepper. Place the potatoes on a plate, top with the rocket and prawns and drizzle with dressing.

Serves 4

Salmon carpaccio

3 vine-ripened tomatoes
1 tablespoon baby capers, rinsed
and drained
1 tablespoon chopped dill
500 g sashimi salmon
1 tablespoon extra virgin olive oil
1 tablespoon lime juice

ciabatta bread

Cut a cross in the base of the tomatoes. Place in a bowl and cover with boiling water. Leave to stand for 2–3 minutes, or until the skin blisters. Drain, plunge into cold water, then drain and peel. Cut the tomatoes in half, scoop out the seeds with a teaspoon and dice the flesh. Place in a bowl and stir in the capers and dill.

Using a very sharp knife, carefully slice the salmon into paper-thin slices, cutting across the grain. Divide the salmon equally among four plates, arranging in a single layer.

Place a mound of the tomato mixture in the centre of each plate. Whisk together the olive oil and lime juice, and season with salt. Drizzle over the tomato and salmon, and season with black pepper. Serve immediately with ciabatta bread.

Serves 4

Artichoke, prosciutto and rocket salad

4 artichokes
2 eggs, lightly beaten
20 g (¼ cup) fresh breadcrumbs
25 g (¼ cup) grated Parmesan
  cheese
olive oil for frying, plus 1 tablespoon
  extra
8 slices prosciutto
3 teaspoons white wine vinegar
1 garlic clove, crushed
150 g rocket, long stalks trimmed

shaved Parmesan cheese (optional)
sea salt

Bring a large saucepan of water to the boil. Remove the hard, outer leaves of each artichoke, trim the stem and cut 2–3 cm off the top. Cut into quarters and remove the furry 'choke'. Boil the pieces for 2 minutes, then drain.

Whisk the eggs in a bowl and combine the seasoned breadcrumbs and grated Parmesan in another bowl. Dip each artichoke quarter into the egg, then roll in the crumb mixture to coat. Fill a frying pan with olive oil to a depth of 2 cm and heat over medium–high heat. Add the artichokes in batches and fry for 2–3 minutes, or until golden. Remove from the pan and drain on paper towels.

Heat 1 tablespoon of olive oil in a non-stick frying pan over medium–high heat. Cook the prosciutto in two batches for 2 minutes, or until crisp and golden. Remove from the pan, reserving the oil.

Combine the reserved oil, vinegar and garlic with a little salt and pepper. Place the rocket in a bowl, add half of the salad dressing and toss well. Divide the rocket, artichokes and prosciutto among four plates, and drizzle with the remaining dressing. Garnish with shaved Parmesan, if desired, and sprinkle with sea salt.

Serves 4

Prawn millefeuille

Lemon mayonnaise
1 egg yolk
½ teaspoon Dijon mustard
pinch of sugar
1 teaspoon cider vinegar
1 teaspoon finely grated lemon zest
1 tablespoon lemon juice
185 ml (¾ cup) oil

2 sheets ready-rolled frozen puff
   pastry, thawed
750 g cooked medium prawns
75 g rocket, torn
½ small red onion, thinly sliced into
   rings
2 tablespoons capers, rinsed
   and drained
1 tablespoon chopped flat-leaf
   parsley

Preheat the oven to 200°C (400°F/ Gas 6) and line two baking trays with baking paper. To make the lemon mayonnaise, combine the egg yolk, mustard, sugar, vinegar, lemon zest and juice in a bowl. Gradually add the oil, at first drop by drop, then in a thin steady stream, beating continuously with a whisk or wooden spoon until it thickens. Season.

Cut the pastry sheets into quarters, then place well apart on the baking trays. Bake for about 15 minutes, or until golden and puffed. Cool for 2 minutes before lifting with a spatula onto a wire rack to cool.

Peel and devein the prawns, then cut them in half lengthways. Using half the rocket, prawns, onion rings and capers, make a neat pile on four serving plates and drizzle with some of the mayonnaise. Place a piece of pastry over the salad, then add the remaining ingredients, including some mayonnaise, on top of the pastry square. Finish with another piece of pastry, sprinkle with parsley and serve.

Serves 4

Haloumi with salad and garlic bread

4 firm, ripe tomatoes
1 Lebanese cucumber
140 g rocket
80 g (1/2 cup) Kalamata olives
1 loaf crusty unsliced white bread
5 tablespoons olive oil
1 large garlic clove, cut in half
400 g haloumi cheese
1 tablespoon lemon juice
1 tablespoon chopped oregano

Preheat the oven to 180°C (350°F/ Gas 4). Heat the grill to high.

Cut the tomatoes and cucumber into bite-sized chunks and place in a serving dish with the rocket and olives. Mix well.

Slice the bread into eight 1.5 cm slices, drizzle 1 1/2 tablespoons of the olive oil over the bread and season with salt and pepper. Grill until lightly golden, then rub each slice thoroughly with a cut side of the garlic. Wrap the bread loosely in foil and keep warm in the oven.

Cut the haloumi into eight slices. Heat 1/2 tablespoon of the oil in a shallow frying pan and fry the haloumi slices for 1–2 minutes on each side, until crisp and golden brown.

Whisk together the lemon juice, oregano and remaining olive oil to use as a dressing. Season, to taste. Pour half the dressing over the salad and toss well. Arrange the haloumi on top and drizzle with dressing. Serve immediately with the warm garlic bread.

Serves 4

Baked ricotta and red capsicum with pesto

1 large red capsicum (pepper), cut
  into quarters and seeded
750 g low-fat ricotta cheese
1 egg
6 slices wholegrain bread

Pesto
2 tablespoons pine nuts
100 g (2 cups) basil
2 garlic cloves
2 tablespoons good-quality olive oil
2 tablespoons finely grated Parmesan
  cheese

Grill the capsicum, skin-side-up, under a hot grill for 5–6 minutes, or until the skin blackens and blisters. Place in a bowl and cover with plastic wrap until cool. Peel off the skin and slice the flesh into 2 cm wide strips.

To make the pesto, place the pine nuts, basil and garlic in a food processor and process for 15 seconds, or until finely chopped. While the processor is running, add the oil in a continuous thin stream, then season with salt and pepper. Stir in the Parmesan.

Preheat the oven to 180°C (350°F/ Gas 4). Grease six large muffin holes.

Mix the ricotta and egg until well combined. Season with salt and freshly ground black pepper. Divide the capsicum strips among the muffin holes, top with 2 teaspoons pesto and spoon in the ricotta mixture.

Bake for 35–40 minutes, or until the ricotta is firm and golden. Cool, then unmould. Toast the bread slices and cut them into fingers. Serve with the baked ricotta and the remaining pesto on the side.

Serves 6

Scallop salad with saffron dressing

pinch saffron threads
60 g (¼ cup) mayonnaise
1½ tablespoons cream
1 teaspoon lemon juice
20 scallops (500 g) with roe
  attached
25 g butter
1 tablespoon olive oil
100 g mixed salad leaves
4 g (⅓ cup) chervil leaves

To make the dressing, place the saffron threads in a bowl and soak in 2 teaspoons of hot water for 10 minutes. Add the mayonnaise, mixing well, until it is a rich yellow in colour. Stir in the cream, then the lemon juice. Refrigerate until needed.

Make sure the scallops are clean of digestive tract before cooking. Heat the butter and olive oil in a large frying pan over high heat and sear the scallops in small batches for 1 minute on each side.

Divide the mixed salad leaves and chervil among four serving plates, then top each with five scallops. Drizzle the dressing over the scallops and the salad leaves before serving.

Serves 4

Orange, goat's cheese and hazelnut salad

20 g hazelnuts
1 tablespoon orange juice
1 tablespoon lemon juice
125 ml (½ cup) olive oil
250 g watercress, well rinsed and
  dried
50 g baby English spinach leaves,
  well rinsed and dried
24 orange segments
300 g firm goat's cheese, sliced into
  4 equal portions

Preheat the oven to 180°C (350°F/ Gas 4). Put the hazelnuts on a tray and roast for 5–6 minutes, or until the skin turns dark brown. Wrap the hazelnuts in a clean tea towel and rub them together to remove the skins.

Combine the nuts, orange juice, lemon juice and a pinch of salt in a food processor. With the motor running, gradually add the oil a few drops at a time. When about half the oil has been added, pour in the remainder in a steady stream.

Remove the stems from the watercress and place the leaves in a bowl with the spinach, orange segments and 2 tablespoons of the dressing. Toss to combine and season to taste with pepper. Arrange the salad on four plates.

Heat a small, non-stick frying pan over medium–high heat and brush lightly with olive oil. When hot, carefully press each slice of goat's cheese firmly into the pan and cook for 1–2 minutes, or until a crust has formed on the cheese. Carefully remove the cheese from the pan and arrange over the salads, crust-side-up. Drizzle the remaining dressing over the salads.

Serves 4

Prawn cocktails

Cocktail sauce
250 g (1 cup) whole-egg mayonnaise
60 ml (¼ cup) tomato sauce
2 teaspoons Worcestershire sauce
½ teaspoon lemon juice
1 drop Tabasco sauce

1 kg cooked medium prawns

lettuce leaves
lemon wedges
sliced bread

For the cocktail sauce, mix all the ingredients together in a bowl and season with salt and pepper.

Peel the prawns, leaving some with their tails intact to use as a garnish. Remove the tails from the rest. Gently pull out the dark vein from each prawn back, starting at the head end. Add the prawns without tails to the sauce and mix to coat.

Arrange lettuce in serving dishes or bowls. Spoon some prawns into each dish. Garnish with the reserved prawns, drizzling with some dressing. Serve with lemon wedges and bread.

Serves 6

Note: If you wish, you can make the cocktail sauce several hours ahead and store it in the refrigerator. Stir in 2 tablespoons of thick (double) cream for a creamier sauce.

Red gazpacho

1 kg vine-ripened tomatoes
2 slices day-old white Italian bread,
  crust removed, broken into pieces
1 red capsicum (pepper), seeded and
  roughly chopped
2 garlic cloves, chopped
1 small green chilli, chopped, optional
1 teaspoon sugar
2 tablespoons red wine vinegar
2 tablespoons extra virgin olive oil
8 ice cubes

Garnish
1/2 Lebanese cucumber, seeded and
  finely diced
1/2 red capsicum (pepper), seeded
  and finely diced
1/2 green capsicum (pepper), seeded
  and finely diced
1/2 red onion, finely diced
1/2 tomato, diced

Score a cross in the base of each tomato. Place in a bowl of boiling water for 1 minute, then plunge into cold water and peel away from the cross. Cut the tomatoes in half, scoop out the seeds and chop the flesh.

Soak the bread in cold water for 5 minutes, then squeeze out any excess liquid. Place the bread in a food processor with the tomato, capsicum, garlic, chilli, sugar and vinegar, and process until smooth.

With the motor running, add the oil to make a smooth mixture. Season with salt and ground black pepper. Refrigerate for at least 2 hours. Add a little extra vinegar, if desired.

To make the garnish, place all the ingredients in a bowl and mix well. Serve the soup in bowls with two ice cubes in each bowl. Spoon the garnish into separate bowls.

Serves 4

Scallops, ginger and spinach salad

300 g scallops, without roe
100 g (2 cups) baby English spinach
  leaves
1 small red capsicum (pepper), cut
  into very fine strips
50 g bean sprouts
25 ml sake
1 tablespoon lime juice
2 teaspoons shaved palm sugar
  or soft brown sugar
1 teaspoon fish sauce

Remove any membrane or hard
white muscle from the scallops.
Lightly brush a chargrill plate with oil.
Cook the scallops in batches on the
chargrill plate for 1 minute each side,
or until cooked.

Divide the spinach, capsicum and
bean sprouts among four plates.
Arrange the scallops over the top.

To make the dressing, place the sake,
lime juice, palm sugar and fish sauce
in a small bowl, and mix together well.
Pour over the salad and serve
immediately.

Serves 4

Asparagus with smoked salmon and hollandaise

175 g butter
4 egg yolks
1 tablespoon lime juice
4 eggs, at room temperature
310 g asparagus spears
200 g smoked salmon
shaved Parmesan cheese

Melt the butter in a small saucepan and skim any froth from the surface. Remove from the heat. In a separate saucepan, mix the egg yolks with 2 tablespoons water. Place over very low heat and whisk for 30 seconds, or until pale and foamy, then continue whisking for 2–3 minutes, or until the whisk leaves a trail — do not overheat the eggs will scramble. Remove from the heat. Add the cooled butter a little at a time, whisking well between each addition. Avoid using the milky whey at the bottom of the pan. Stir in the lime juice and season. If the sauce is still runny, return to the heat and whisk vigorously until thick, taking care not to scramble.

Half fill a saucepan with water and add the eggs. Bring to the boil and cook for 6–7 minutes, stirring occasionally to centre the yolks. Drain and cool, then peel and quarter.

Bring a large saucepan of lightly salted water to the boil. Add the asparagus and cook for 3 minutes, or until just tender. Drain and pat dry. Divide the asparagus and smoked salmon among four serving plates. Arrange the eggs over the top. Spoon on the hollandaise and top with the Parmesan. Season and serve.

Serves 4

Haloumi and asparagus salad with salsa verde

250 g haloumi cheese
380 g small, thin asparagus spears
2 tablespoons garlic oil
7 g (¼ cup) basil leaves
10 g (½ cup) mint leaves
20 g (1 cup) parsley leaves
2 tablespoons baby capers rinsed
  and drained
1 garlic clove
2 tablespoons olive oil
1 tablespoon lemon juice
1 tablespoon lime juice
2 handfuls mixed salad leaves

Heat a chargrill pan over medium heat. Cut the haloumi into 1 cm slices and cut each slice in half diagonally to make two small triangles. Brush the haloumi and asparagus with the garlic oil. Chargrill the asparagus for 1 minute or until just tender, and the haloumi until grill marks appear and it is warmed through. Keep warm.

To make the salsa verde, place the herbs, capers, garlic and oil in a food processor and blend until smooth. Add the juices, and pulse briefly.

Divide the salad leaves among four serving plates. Top with the haloumi and asparagus, and drizzle with a little salsa verde.

Serves 4

Sweet citrus scallop salad

Lemon and herb dressing
½ preserved lemon
60 ml (¼ cup) olive oil
2 tablespoons lemon juice
1 tablespoon sweet chilli sauce
2 tablespoons white wine vinegar
2 tablespoons chopped coriander

500 g potatoes
oil, for shallow-frying
750 g scallops, without roe
2 tablespoons olive oil, extra
75 g baby English spinach leaves

For the dressing, scoop out and discard the pulp from the preserved lemon, wash the skin and cut into thin slices. Put in a bowl and whisk with the olive oil, lemon juice, sweet chilli sauce, wine vinegar and coriander.

Cut the potatoes into paper-thin slices. Heat 2 cm oil in a deep heavy-based frying pan and cook batches of the potato for 1–2 minutes, or until crisp and golden. Drain on crumpled paper towels.

Slice or pull off any membrane, vein or hard white muscle from the scallops. Heat the extra oil in a frying pan over high heat and cook the scallops in batches for 1–2 minutes, or until they are golden brown on both sides.

Divide half the spinach among four plates. Top with potato, then half the scallops and more spinach. Finish with more scallops. Drizzle with the dressing just before serving.

Serves 4

Smoked salmon and rocket salad

Dressing
1 tablespoon extra virgin olive oil
2 tablespoons balsamic vinegar

150 g rocket
1 avocado
250 g smoked salmon
325 g jar marinated goat's cheese,
  drained and crumbled
2 tablespoons roasted hazelnuts,
  coarsely chopped

For the dressing, thoroughly whisk together the oil and vinegar in a bowl. Season, to taste.

Trim any long stems from the rocket, rinse, pat dry and gently toss in a bowl with the dressing.

Cut the avocado in half lengthways, then cut each half lengthways into six wedges. Discard the skin and place three wedges on each serving plate and arrange a pile of rocket over the top.

Drape pieces of salmon over the rocket. Scatter the cheese and nuts over the top and season with ground black pepper. Serve immediately.

Serves 4

Note: A whole smoked trout can be used instead of the salmon. Peel, remove the bones, then break the flesh into bite-sized pieces.

Vietnamese prawn salad

1 small Chinese cabbage, finely
  shredded
60 g (¼ cup) sugar
60 ml (¼ cup) fish sauce
80 ml (⅓ cup) lime juice
1 tablespoon white vinegar
1 small red onion, finely sliced
750 g fresh cooked tiger prawns,
  peeled and deveined, tails intact
30 g (⅔ cup) chopped coriander
  leaves
30 g (⅔ cup) chopped Vietnamese
  mint leaves

Vietnamese mint leaves

Place the Chinese cabbage in a large
bowl, cover with plastic wrap and chill
for 30 minutes.

Put the sugar, fish sauce, lime juice,
vinegar and ½ teaspoon salt in a
small jug and mix well.

Toss together the shredded cabbage,
onion, prawns, coriander, mint and
dressing, and garnish with the extra
mint leaves.

Serves 6

Note: Vietnamese mint is available
from Asian grocery stores.

Mains

Lamb with roasted tomatoes

1 tablespoon red wine vinegar
½ Lebanese cucumber, finely diced
100 g Greek-style yoghurt
2 teaspoons chopped mint
½ teaspoon ground cumin
80 ml (⅓ cup) olive oil
6 vine-ripened tomatoes
4 garlic cloves, finely chopped
1 tablespoon chopped oregano
1 tablespoon chopped parsley
600 g asparagus spears, trimmed
2 lamb backstraps or fillets (500 g)

Combine the vinegar, cucumber, yoghurt, chopped mint, cumin and 1 tablespoon of olive oil in a small jug.

Preheat the oven to 180°C (350°F/ Gas 4). Cut the tomatoes in half and scoop out the seeds. Combine the garlic, oregano and parsley, and sprinkle into the tomato shells.

Place the tomatoes on a rack in a baking tin. Drizzle them with 1 tablespoon of the olive oil and roast for 1 hour. Remove from the oven, cut each piece in half again and keep warm. Place the asparagus in the roasting tin, drizzle with another tablespoon of olive oil, season and roast for 10 minutes.

Meanwhile, heat the remaining oil in a frying pan. Season the lamb well and cook over medium–high heat for 5 minutes on each side, then set aside to rest.

Remove the asparagus from the oven and arrange on a serving plate. Top with the tomato. Slice the lamb on the diagonal and arrange on top of the tomato. Drizzle with the dressing and serve immediately.

Serves 4

Indian marinated chicken salad

60 ml (¼ cup) lemon juice
1½ teaspoons garam masala
1 teaspoon ground turmeric
1 tablespoon finely grated fresh
  ginger
2 garlic cloves, finely chopped
3½ tablespoons vegetable oil
3 chicken breast fillets (650 g)
1 onion, thinly sliced
2 zucchini (courgettes), thinly sliced
  on the diagonal
100 g watercress leaves
150 g freshly shelled peas
2 ripe tomatoes, finely chopped
30 g (1 cup) coriander leaves

Dressing
1 teaspoon cumin seeds
½ teaspoon coriander seeds
90 g (⅓ cup) natural yoghurt
2 tablespoons chopped mint
2 tablespoons lemon juice

Combine the lemon juice, garam masala, turmeric, ginger, garlic and 2 teaspoons oil in a large bowl. Add the chicken fillets and onion, toss to coat in the marinade, cover, and refrigerate for 1 hour.

Remove and discard the onion then heat 2 tablespoons of oil in a large, frying pan. Cook the chicken for about 4–5 minutes on each side or until it is cooked through. Remove the chicken from the pan and leave for 5 minutes. Cut each breast across the grain into 1 cm slices.

Heat the remaining oil in the pan and cook the zucchini for 2 minutes, or until lightly golden and tender. Toss with the watercress in a large bowl. Cook the peas in boiling water for 5 minutes, or until tender, then drain. Rinse under cold water to cool. Add to the salad with the tomato, chicken and coriander.

For the dressing, gently roast the cumin and coriander seeds in a dry frying pan for 1–2 minutes, or until fragrant. Remove, then pound the seeds to a powder. Mix with the yoghurt, mint and lemon juice, then gently fold through the salad.

Serves 4

White bean salad with tuna

200 g (1 cup) dried cannellini beans
  (see Note)
2 fresh bay leaves
1 large garlic clove, smashed
350 g green beans, trimmed
2 baby fennel bulbs, thinly sliced
½ small red onion, very thinly sliced
30 g (1 cup) parsley leaves, roughly
  chopped
1 tablespoon olive oil
2 fresh tuna fillets (400 g)
80 ml (⅓ cup) lemon juice
1 garlic clove, extra, finely chopped
1 red chilli, seeds removed, finely
  chopped
1 teaspoon sugar
1 tablespoon lemon zest
125 ml (½ cup) extra virgin olive oil

Put the beans in a bowl, cover with cold water, allowing room for the beans to expand, and leave for at least 8 hours.

Rinse the beans well and transfer them to a saucepan. Cover with cold water, add the torn bay leaves and smashed garlic, and simmer for 20–25 minutes, or until tender. Drain.

Cook the green beans in boiling water for 1–2 minutes, or until tender, and refresh under cold water. Mix with the fennel, onion and parsley.

Heat the oil in a large, heavy-based frying pan and cook the tuna fillets over high heat for 2 minutes on each side or until still pink in the centre. Remove, rest for 2–3 minutes, then cut into 3 cm chunks. Add to the green bean mixture with the cannellini beans and toss to combine.

Combine the lemon juice, garlic, chilli, sugar and lemon zest. Whisk in the olive oil and season with salt and pepper. Toss gently through the salad.

Serves 4–6

Note: You may substitute a 425 g tin of cooked cannellini beans for the dried beans. Rinse and drain well before using — they will not require any further preparation.

Minced pork and noodle salad

1 tablespoon peanut oil
500 g minced pork
2 garlic cloves, finely chopped
1 stalk lemon grass, finely chopped
2–3 red Asian shallots, thinly sliced
3 teaspoons finely grated fresh ginger
1 small red chilli, finely chopped
5 fresh kaffir lime leaves, very finely
  shredded
170 g glass (mung bean) noodles
60 g baby English spinach leaves
50 g (1 cup) roughly chopped
  coriander
170 g peeled, finely chopped fresh
  pineapple
10 g (1/2 cup) mint leaves
1 1/2 tablespoons shaved palm sugar
  or soft brown sugar
2 tablespoons fish sauce
80 ml (1/3 cup) lime juice
2 teaspoons sesame oil
2 teaspoons peanut oil, extra

Heat a wok until very hot, add the peanut oil and swirl to coat the wok. Add the pork and stir-fry in batches over high heat for 5 minutes, or until lightly golden. Add the garlic, lemon grass, shallots, grated ginger, chilli and lime leaves, and stir-fry for a further 1–2 minutes, or until fragrant.

Place the noodles in a large bowl and cover with boiling water for 30 seconds, or until softened. Rinse under cold water and drain well. Toss in a bowl with the spinach, coriander, pineapple, mint and pork mixture.

To make the dressing, mix together the palm sugar, fish sauce and lime juice. Add the sesame oil and extra peanut oil, and whisk to combine. Toss through the salad and season with freshly ground black pepper.

Serves 4

Warm chicken and pasta salad

375 g penne
100 ml olive oil
4 long, thin eggplants (aubergines),
    thinly sliced on the diagonal
2 chicken breast fillets
2 teaspoons lemon juice
15 g (½ cup) chopped flat-leaf parsley
270 g chargrilled red capsicum
    (pepper), drained and sliced
    (see Note)
155 g fresh asparagus spears,
    trimmed, blanched and cut into
    5 cm lengths
85 g semi-dried (sun-blushed)
    tomatoes, finely sliced

grated Parmesan cheese (optional)

Cook the pasta in a large saucepan of boiling water until *al dente*. Drain, return to the pan and keep warm. Heat 2 tablespoons of the oil in a large frying pan over high heat and cook the eggplant for 4–5 minutes, or until golden and cooked through.

Heat a lightly oiled chargrill pan over high heat and cook the chicken for 5 minutes each side, or until browned and cooked through. Cut into thick slices. Combine the lemon juice, parsley and the remaining oil in a small jar and shake well. Return the pasta to the heat, toss through the dressing, chicken, eggplant, capsicum, asparagus and tomato until well mixed and warmed through. Season with black pepper. Serve warm with a scattering of grated Parmesan, if desired.

Serves 4

Note: Jars of chargrilled capsicum can be bought at the supermarket; otherwise, visit your local deli.

Greek peppered lamb salad

300 g lamb backstraps or fillets
1 1/2 tablespoons black pepper
3 vine-ripened tomatoes, cut into
   8 wedges
2 Lebanese cucumbers, sliced
150 g lemon and garlic marinated
   Kalamata olives, drained (reserving
   1 1/2 tablespoons oil)
100 g Greek feta cheese, cubed
3/4 teaspoon dried oregano
1 tablespoon lemon juice
1 tablespoon extra virgin olive oil

Roll the backstraps in the pepper, pressing the pepper on with your fingers. Cover and refrigerate for 15 minutes.

Place the tomato, cucumber, olives, feta and 1/2 teaspoon of the dried oregano in a bowl.

Heat a chargrill pan or barbecue plate, brush with oil and when very hot, cook the lamb for 2–3 minutes on each side, or until cooked to your liking. Keep warm.

Whisk the lemon juice, extra virgin olive oil, reserved Kalamata oil and the remaining dried oregano together well. Season. Pour half the dressing over the salad, toss together and arrange on a serving platter.

Cut the lamb on the diagonal into 1 cm thick slices and arrange on top of the salad. Pour the remaining dressing on top and serve.

Serves 4

Chargrilled chicken with spinach and raspberries

60 ml (¼ cup) raspberry vinegar
2 tablespoons lime juice
2 garlic cloves, crushed
2 tablespoons chopped oregano
1 teaspoon soft brown sugar
2 small red chillies, finely chopped
125 ml (½ cup) virgin olive oil
4 chicken breast fillets
1 teaspoon Dijon mustard
200 g baby English spinach leaves
250 g fresh raspberries

Mix 2 tablespoons of the raspberry vinegar, the lime juice, crushed garlic, 1 tablespoon of the oregano, the sugar, chilli and 60 ml (¼ cup) of the oil in a large bowl. Immerse the chicken in the marinade, cover and refrigerate for 2 hours.

Preheat the oven to 180°C (350°F/ Gas 4). Heat a chargrill pan and cook the chicken for 3 minutes on each side, then place on a baking tray and bake for a further 5 minutes, or until cooked through. Allow the chicken to rest for 5 minutes, then cut each breast into five strips on the diagonal.

To make the dressing, combine the remaining oil, vinegar and oregano with the mustard, ¼ teaspoon salt and freshly ground black pepper and mix well. Toss the spinach and raspberries with half of the dressing. Top with the chicken and drizzle with the remaining dressing.

Serves 4

Fusilli salad with sherry vinaigrette

300 g fusilli
250 g (2 cups) cauliflower florets
125 ml (½ cup) olive oil
16 slices pancetta
10 g (½ cup) small sage leaves
100 g (⅔ cup) pine nuts, toasted
2 tablespoons finely chopped Asian shallots
1½ tablespoons sherry vinegar
1 small red chilli, finely chopped
2 garlic cloves, crushed
1 teaspoon soft brown sugar
2 tablespoons orange juice
15 g (¼ cup) parsley, finely chopped
35 g (⅓ cup) shaved Parmesan cheese

Cook the fusilli in a large saucepan of rapidly boiling, salted water for 12 minutes, or until *al dente*. Drain and refresh under cold water until it is cool. Drain well. Blanch the cauliflower florets in boiling water for 3 minutes, then drain and cool.

Heat 1 tablespoon of olive oil in a non-stick frying pan and cook the pancetta for 2 minutes or until crisp. Drain on crumpled paper towels. Add 1 more tablespoon of oil and cook the sage leaves for 1 minute or until crisp. Drain on crumpled paper towels. In a large serving bowl, combine the pasta, pine nuts and cauliflower.

Heat the remaining olive oil, add the shallots and cook gently for 2 minutes, or until soft. Remove from the heat then add the vinegar, chilli, garlic, brown sugar, orange juice and chopped parsley. Pour the warm dressing over the pasta and toss gently to combine.

Place the salad in a serving bowl. Crumble the pancetta over the top and scatter with sage leaves and shaved Parmesan. Serve warm.

Serves 6

Prawn tacos

2 firm ripe tomatoes, seeded and
  diced
2 tablespoons lime juice
1/2 teaspoon chilli powder
1/2 teaspoon ground cumin
2 tablespoons oil
1 red onion, diced
4 garlic cloves, crushed
18 raw medium prawns, peeled,
  deveined and roughly chopped
3 tablespoons chopped flat-leaf
  parsley
8 corn taco shells
150 g shredded iceberg lettuce
1 avocado, diced
125 g (1/2 cup) sour cream

Preheat the oven to 180°C (350°F/
Gas 4). Combine the tomato, lime
juice, chilli powder and cumin.

Heat the oil in a frying pan, add the
onion and garlic and cook gently for
3–5 minutes, or until soft. Add the
prawns and toss briefly, then stir
in the tomato mixture and cook
for another 3–5 minutes, or until
the prawns are pink and cooked. Stir
in the parsley. Meanwhile, heat the
taco shells on a baking tray in the
oven for 5 minutes.

Place some lettuce in the bottom
of each taco shell, then fill with
the prawn mixture. Top with some
avocado and a dollop of sour cream.

Serves 4

Warm pork salad with blue cheese croutons

125 ml (½ cup) olive oil
1 large garlic clove, crushed
400 g pork fillet, cut into 5 mm slices
1 small or ½ a large baguette, cut
  into 20 x 5 mm slices
100 g blue cheese, crumbled
2 tablespoons sherry vinegar
½ teaspoon soft brown sugar
150 g mixed salad leaves

Place the olive oil and garlic in a jar and shake well. Heat 2 teaspoons of the garlic oil in a frying pan, add half the pork and cook for 1 minute on each side. Remove and keep warm. Add another 2 teaspoons garlic oil and cook the remaining pork. Remove. Season the pork with salt and black pepper to taste.

Lay the bread slices on a baking tray and brush with a little garlic oil on one side. Cook the bread under a hot grill until golden. Turn the bread over, sprinkle with the crumbled blue cheese, then return to the grill and cook until the cheese has melted (this will happen very quickly).

Add the sherry vinegar and sugar to the remaining garlic oil and shake well. Place the salad leaves in a large bowl, add the pork and pour on the salad dressing. Toss well. Place a mound of salad in the middle of four serving plates and arrange five croutons around the edge of each salad. Serve the salad immediately.

Serves 4

Thai beef salad

600 g beef fillet, trimmed
125 ml (½ cup) fish sauce
1 tablespoon peanut oil
1 small dried red chilli, roughly
　chopped
4 Asian shallots, finely sliced
2 spring onions, thinly sliced on an
　angle
4 tablespoons mint leaves
4 tablespoons coriander leaves
1 garlic clove, crushed
100 ml lime juice
2 teaspoons grated palm sugar or
　soft brown sugar
2 vine-ripened tomatoes, each cut
　into 8 wedges
100 g butter lettuce, washed and
　trimmed

Place the beef fillet in a bowl with
2 tablespoons of fish sauce. Cover
and chill for 3 hours, turning the
meat several times.

Place a baking tray in the oven and
preheat to 220°C (425°F/ Gas 7).
Heat the oil in a frying pan over
high heat and cook the beef fillet
for 1 minute on each side, or until
browned, then roast for 15 minutes,
or until medium–rare. Remove from
the oven and rest for 10 minutes.

Meanwhile, place the chilli in a small,
non-stick frying pan over medium–
high heat. Dry-fry for 1–2 minutes,
or until the chilli is dark but not burnt.
Transfer to a mortar and pestle or
spice mill, and grind until fine. Mix
the ground chilli in a bowl with the
shallots, spring onion, mint, coriander,
garlic, lime juice, palm sugar and
remaining fish sauce, stirring to
dissolve the sugar if necessary.

Cut the beef into thin strips and
place in a bowl with the dressing
and tomato. Toss well. Arrange the
lettuce on a serving platter and pile
the beef salad on top.

Serves 4

Fresh salmon patties with mango salsa

1 garlic clove, peeled
500 g fresh salmon, skin removed,
  roughly chopped
1 red onion, diced
50 g (½ cup) dry breadcrumbs
1 egg
50 g (1 cup) chopped coriander
1 mango, diced
60 ml (¼ cup) lime juice

Place the garlic, salmon and half the onion in a food processor and process until coarsely minced. Add the breadcrumbs, egg and half the coriander, and season. Mix together well and divide into six equal portions. Shape into patties, place on a plate, cover and refrigerate for 30 minutes. To make the salsa, place the mango, 2 tablespoons lime juice and the remaining onion and coriander in a bowl, and mix together well.

Heat a lightly greased non-stick frying pan, add the remaining lime juice and cook the patties for 4–5 minutes each side. They should be moist and slightly pink inside. To serve, place the patties on six serving plates and spoon over the salsa.

Serves 6

Note: The patties can be served between foccacia with salad greens, or with a salad and bread on the side. If unavailable, fresh salmon can be replaced by tinned salmon.

Mediterranean layered cob

2 eggplants (aubergines)
4 zucchini (courgettes)
900 g orange sweet potato
2 large red capsicums (peppers)
80 ml (⅓ cup) olive oil
23 cm round cob loaf
165 g jar pesto
200 g ricotta cheese
35 g (⅓ cup) grated Parmesan
  cheese

Cut the eggplant and zucchini into 1 cm slices lengthways. Sprinkle the eggplant with salt and drain for 30 minutes, then rinse and pat dry.

Cut the sweet potato into 5 mm slices. Quarter the capsicums and remove the seeds and membranes. Grill, skin-side-up, until the skins have blackened. Leave to cool in a plastic bag, then remove the skins. Brush the eggplant, sweet potato and zucchini with olive oil and chargrill, in batches, until lightly browned.

Cut a lid from the top of the loaf. Remove the bread from inside, leaving a 1 cm shell. Brush the inside of the loaf and lid with pesto. Layer the zucchini and capsicum inside the loaf, then spread with the combined ricotta and Parmesan. Layer in the sweet potato and eggplant, lightly pressing down to fit. Replace the lid.

Cover the loaf with plastic wrap and place on a baking tray. Place another tray on top and put heavy food tins on top of the tray. Chill overnight.

Preheat the oven to 250°C (500°F/ Gas 9). Remove the plastic wrap, return the loaf to the baking tray and bake for about 10 minutes, or until crispy. Cut into wedges to serve.

Serves 6

Salami pasta salad

1 red capsicum (pepper)
1 green capsicum (pepper)
4 celery stalks
1 fennel bulb, trimmed
1 red onion
200 g thickly sliced pepper-coated
  salami
15 g (½ cup) chopped flat-leaf parsley
300 g mixed coloured fettucine,
  broken into short pieces

Dressing
125 ml (½ cup) olive oil
3 tablespoons lemon juice
2½ tablespoons Dijon mustard
1 teaspoon sugar
1 garlic clove, crushed

Slice the red and green capsicums into strips and place them in a large bowl. Slice the celery and add to the bowl. Cut the fennel and onion in half, then slice and add to the bowl. Cut the salami into strips and add to the bowl along with the parsley.

Cook the fettucine in a large pan of rapidly boiling salted water until just tender. Drain and rinse in cold water. Transfer the cooked pasta to the bowl and mix thoroughly with the capsicum, celery, fennel, onion, parsley and salami.

To make the dressing, combine the olive oil, lemon juice, mustard, sugar and crushed garlic, and season to taste with salt and plenty of cracked pepper. Pour over the salad and toss well to coat.

Serves 8

Prawn skewers with coconut sambal

80 ml (1/3 cup) coconut cream
60 ml (1/4 cup) lime juice
2 tablespoons soy sauce
1 tablespoon grated lime zest
2 teaspoons chopped red chilli
1 teaspoon grated palm sugar
　or soft brown sugar
1/2 teaspoon shrimp paste
4 garlic cloves, crushed
32 raw medium prawns, peeled and
　deveined, with tails intact
2 teaspoons oil
1 tablespoon chopped coriander

mango chutney

Coconut sambal
25 g (1/4 cup) desiccated coconut
40 g (1/4 cup) sesame seeds
1/2 teaspoon dried garlic flakes
1/4 teaspoon ground coriander
1/4 teaspoon ground cumin
40 g (1/4 cup) roasted unsalted
　peanuts, roughly chopped

Soak eight bamboo skewers in water for 30 minutes.

Combine the coconut cream, lime juice, soy sauce, lime zest, chilli, sugar, shrimp paste and garlic and mix until the sugar dissolves.

Thread four prawns on each skewer. Place on a non-metallic plate and pour the marinade over them and refrigerate, covered, for 1 hour.

To make the sambal, toast the coconut in a dry frying pan for 1–2 minutes, or until golden, then add the sesame seeds, garlic flakes, spices and 1/2 teaspoon salt and cook for about 30 seconds. Remove from the heat and stir in the peanuts. Spoon into a small serving bowl.

Heat a chargrill pan or barbecue to high and brush with a little oil. Cook the prawns on both sides for 2–3 minutes, or until pink and cooked. Place on a platter and sprinkle with coriander. Serve with the sambal and chutney.

Serves 4

Roast beef and spinach salad with horseradish

200 g green beans, trimmed
500 g rump steak, cut into 3 cm
   thick pieces
1 red onion, peeled and halved
1 tablespoon olive oil
100 g (2¼ cups) baby spinach
50 g (1½ cups) watercress leaves
200 g semi-dried (sun-blushed)
   tomatoes
125 g (½ cup) plain Greek-style
   yoghurt
1 tablespoon creamed horseradish
2 tablespoons lemon juice
2 tablespoons cream
2 garlic cloves
2–3 dashes Tabasco sauce

sea salt, to taste

Bring a saucepan of water to the boil, add the beans and cook for 4 minutes, or until tender. Drain, and refresh under cold water. When cool, drain and set aside. Preheat a grill or barbecue. Brush the steak and onion with oil, and cook the steak for 2 minutes each side, or until rare. Remove the steak and leave for 5 minutes. Meanwhile, cook the onion for 2–3 minutes each side, or until charred.

Place the spinach, watercress, tomatoes and beans in a large salad bowl. In a small bowl, whisk together the yoghurt, horseradish, lemon juice, cream, garlic, Tabasco and some black pepper to taste. Chill for 15 minutes.

Slice the beef thinly across the grain, and layer carefully over the salad. Slice the grilled onion, add to the salad and drizzle with the dressing. Season well with sea salt and freshly ground black pepper.

Serves 4

Note: This cooking time will result in rare beef. Cook for a little longer if you prefer your beef medium or well done.

Caesar salad

3 eggs
3 garlic cloves, crushed
2–3 anchovy fillets
1 teaspoon Worcestershire sauce
2 tablespoons lime juice
1 teaspoon Dijon mustard
185 ml (¾ cup) olive oil
3 slices white bread
20 g butter
1 tablespoon oil, extra
3 rashers back bacon
1 large or 4 baby cos lettuces
75 g (¾ cup) shaved Parmesan
  cheese

Process the eggs, garlic, anchovies, Worcestershire sauce, lime juice and mustard in a food processor until smooth. With the motor running, add the oil in a thin, continuous stream to produce a creamy dressing. Season to taste with salt and freshly ground black pepper.

Cut the crusts off the bread, then cut the bread into 1.5 cm cubes. Heat the butter and extra olive oil in a frying pan over medium heat, add the bread and cook for 5–8 minutes, or until crisp, then remove from the pan. Cook the bacon in the same pan for 3 minutes, or until it is crispy, then break into bite-sized pieces.

Toss the lettuce leaves with the dressing, then stir in the croutons and bacon, and top with Parmesan.

Serves 4–6

Tequila and lime grilled prawns

32 raw large prawns
125 ml (½ cup) lime juice
60 ml (¼ cup) tequila
2 small red chillies, finely chopped
3 tablespoons chopped coriander
2 tablespoons olive oil
2 garlic cloves, crushed

Green tomato salsa
1 green tomato, seeded and diced
2 tablespoons finely chopped red
   onion
2 green chillies, seeded and finely
   diced
25 g (½ cup) chopped coriander

1 garlic clove, chopped
1 tablespoon olive oil
1 avocado
1 tablespoon lime juice

Soak eight wooden skewers in cold water for 30 minutes. Peel and devein the prawns, leaving the tails intact. Thread four prawns onto each skewer. Lay out the skewers in a single layer in a non-metallic dish.

Combine the lime juice, tequila, chilli, coriander, oil and garlic in a small jug, then pour over the prawns. Cover and marinate in the fridge for 30 minutes.

To make the salsa, mix together the tomato, onion, chilli, coriander, garlic and olive oil, then season. Cover and refrigerate until needed.

Cook the skewers on a hot lightly oiled chargrill pan or barbecue hotplate for 3–5 minutes, or until pink and cooked through, brushing with the marinade during cooking to keep the prawns moist.

Before serving, halve the avocado, remove the stone, cut the flesh into 1 cm dice, then gently mix the avocado into the salsa, stirring in the lime juice at the same time. Season to taste, then serve with the prawns.

Serves 4

Lamb, capsicum and cucumber salad

1 red onion, very thinly sliced
1 red capsicum (pepper), very thinly
  sliced
1 green capsicum (pepper), very thinly
  sliced
2 large Lebanese cucumbers, cut into
  batons
20 g (1/3 cup) shredded mint
3 tablespoons chopped dill
60 ml (1/4 cup) olive oil
600 g lamb backstraps or fillets
80 ml (1/3 cup) lemon juice
2 small garlic cloves, crushed
100 ml extra virgin olive oil

Combine the onion, red and green capsicum, cucumber, mint and dill in a large bowl.

Heat a chargrill pan or frying pan until hot. Drizzle with the oil and cook the lamb for 2–3 minutes on each side, or until it is tender but still a little pink. Remove from the pan and allow to rest for 5 minutes. Thinly slice the lamb and add to the salad, tossing to mix.

Combine the lemon juice and garlic in a small jug, then whisk in the extra virgin olive oil with a fork until well combined. Season with salt and black pepper, then toss the dressing gently through the salad.

Serves 4

Note: This salad is delicious served on fresh or toasted Turkish bread spread with hummus.

Brown rice and puy lentils with pine nuts and spinach

200 g (1 cup) brown rice
100 ml extra virgin olive oil
1 red onion, diced
2 garlic cloves, crushed
1 carrot, diced
2 celery stalks, diced
185 g (1 cup) puy lentils (see Note)
2 tomatoes, seeded and diced
3 tablespoons chopped coriander
3 tablespoons chopped mint
2 tablespoons balsamic vinegar
1 tablespoon lemon juice
2 tablespoons toasted pine nuts
90 g (2 cups) baby spinach leaves,
   washed

Bring a large saucepan of water to the boil. Add 1 teaspoon salt and the rice, and cook for 20 minutes, or until tender. Drain and refresh under cold running water.

Heat 2 tablespoons oil in a saucepan and add the onion, garlic, carrot and celery. Cook over low heat for 5 minutes, or until softened, then add the puy lentils and 375 ml (1½ cups) water. Bring to the boil and simmer for 15 minutes, or until tender. Drain well, but do not rinse. Combine with the rice, tomato, coriander and mint in a large bowl.

Whisk the remaining oil with the balsamic vinegar and lemon juice, and season well with salt and freshly ground black pepper. Pour over the salad, add the pine nuts and the spinach, and toss well to combine.

Serves 6–8

Note: Puy lentils are green French lentils available at specialist food stores and some supermarkets. You can use green or brown lentils instead.

Risoni and broccoli salad with fresh herb dressing

8 garlic cloves, unpeeled
2 tablespoons extra virgin olive oil
125 g whole egg mayonnaise
100 g crème fraîche
80 g pesto
2 tablespoons lemon juice
250 g broccoli florets
400 g risoni (rice-shaped pasta)
100 g toasted slivered almonds
1 tablespoon finely chopped parsley
1 tablespoon finely chopped chives

shaved Parmesan cheese

Preheat the oven to 180°C (350°F/ Gas 4). Toss the garlic cloves in the olive oil and bake for 45 minutes, or until they are soft and golden.

Squeeze two of the garlic cloves from their skins and place in a food processor. Add the mayonnaise, crème fraîche, pesto and lemon juice, and process until just combined, then set aside until required.

Meanwhile, steam the broccoli florets for a few minutes, then refresh under cold water and drain well. Bring a large saucepan of water to the boil, then add 1 teaspoon of salt and the risoni, and cook for 8–10 minutes, or until *al dente*. Drain.

Add the almonds, dressing, parsley and chives to the risoni while still warm, and toss with the broccoli in a large bowl. Serve in deep salad bowls garnished with shaved Parmesan and a roasted garlic clove on each portion.

Serves 6

Variation: Adding some cooked, peeled king prawns will make this salad extra special.

Beef satay salad

2 teaspoons tamarind pulp
1/2 teaspoon sesame oil
2 tablespoons soy sauce
2 teaspoons soft brown sugar
2 garlic cloves, crushed
1 tablespoon lime juice
700 g rump steak
1 tablespoon peanut oil
6 large cos lettuce leaves, washed,
   dried and shredded
1 red capsicum (pepper), julienned
180 g (2 cups) bean sprouts
2 tablespoons fried onion flakes

Satay sauce
2 red chillies, chopped
1/2 teaspoon shrimp paste
1 garlic clove
6 red Asian shallots
2 teaspoons peanut oil
250 ml (1 cup) coconut milk
1 tablespoon lime juice
120 g (3/4 cup) unsalted roasted
   peanuts, finely ground in a food
   processor
1 tablespoon kecap manis
1 tablespoon soft brown sugar
1 tablespoon fish sauce
2 kaffir lime leaves, shredded

Combine the tamarind pulp and 60 ml (1/4 cup) of boiling water and allow to cool. Mash the pulp with your fingertips to dissolve it, then strain, reserving the liquid. Discard the pulp.

Put the sesame oil, soy sauce, sugar, garlic, lime juice and 2 tablespoons of tamarind water in a large bowl. Add the steak, turn to coat, and cover with plastic wrap. Chill for 2 hours.

Meanwhile, to make the satay sauce, process the chillies, shrimp paste, garlic and shallots to a paste in a food processor. Heat the oil in a frying pan and cook the paste for 3 minutes. Add the coconut milk, lime juice, ground peanuts, remaining tamarind water, kecap manis, sugar, fish sauce and kaffir lime leaves. Cook over medium heat until thickened. Thin with 125 ml (1/2 cup) water, and return to the boil for 2 minutes. Season.

Heat the peanut oil in a frying pan over high heat, and cook the steak for 3 minutes on each side, or until medium–rare. Leave for 3 minutes, then thinly slice. Toss the steak slices in a large bowl with the lettuce, capsicum and bean sprouts. Pile onto serving plates, drizzle with the satay sauce, and sprinkle with the fried onion flakes.

Serves 4

Crab salad with green mango and coconut

2 garlic cloves, peeled
2 small red chillies
2 tablespoons dried shrimp
2 tablespoons fish sauce
3 tablespoons lime juice
3 teaspoons palm sugar or soft
  brown sugar
30 g ($\frac{1}{2}$ cup) shredded coconut
  (see Notes)
300 g (1$\frac{1}{2}$ cups) shredded green
  mango
10 g ($\frac{1}{2}$ cup) mint leaves (torn if
  very big)
15 g ($\frac{1}{2}$ cup) coriander leaves
3 kaffir lime leaves, shredded
2 teaspoons thinly shredded, pickled
  ginger
500 g fresh crabmeat

banana leaves, optional
crushed toasted peanuts
lime wedges

Preheat the oven to 180°C (350°F/ Gas 4). Place the garlic, chillies, dried shrimp and $\frac{1}{2}$ teaspoon salt in a mortar and pestle. Pound to a paste, then whisk in the fish sauce, lime juice and palm sugar with a fork.

Place the shredded coconut on a baking tray and bake for 3–5 minutes, shaking the tray occasionally to ensure even toasting. Watch the coconut closely, as it will burn easily.

Place the shredded mango in a large bowl and add the mint, coriander, kaffir lime leaves, ginger, coconut and crabmeat. Pour on the dressing and toss together gently.

Place a piece of banana leaf (if using) in each serving bowl. Mound some crab salad on top, sprinkle with the peanuts and serve immediately with lime wedges.

Serves 4–6

Notes: Freshly shredded coconut is delicious, so if you have the time, remove the skin from a coconut and shred using a vegetable peeler. The banana leaves are for presentation only, and are not edible.

Spicy lamb and noodle salad

1 tablespoon five-spice powder
60 ml (¼ cup) vegetable oil
2 garlic cloves, crushed
2 lamb backstraps or fillets (about
    250 g each)
500 g fresh Shanghai (wheat) noodles
1½ teaspoons sesame oil
80 g snow pea (mangetout) sprouts
½ red capsicum (pepper), thinly sliced
4 spring onions, thinly sliced on the
    diagonal
2 tablespoons sesame seeds, toasted

Dressing
1 tablespoon finely chopped fresh
    ginger
1 tablespoon Chinese black vinegar
1 tablespoon Chinese rice wine
2 tablespoons peanut oil
2 teaspoons chilli oil

Combine the five-spice powder, 2 tablespoons of the vegetable oil and garlic in a large bowl. Add the lamb and turn to coat well. Cover and marinate for 30 minutes.

Cook the noodles in a large saucepan of boiling water for 4–5 minutes, or until tender. Drain, rinse with cold water and drain again. Add the sesame oil and toss to combine.

Heat the remaining vegetable oil in a large frying pan. Cook the lamb over medium–high heat for 3 minutes each side for medium–rare, or until cooked to your liking. Rest for 5 minutes, then thinly slice across the grain.

To make the dressing, combine the ginger, Chinese black vinegar, rice wine, peanut oil and chilli oil.

Place the noodles, lamb strips, snow pea sprouts, capsicum, spring onion and the dressing in a large bowl and toss gently until well combined. Sprinkle with the sesame seeds and serve immediately.

Serves 4

Crab, Camembert and fusilli frittata

80 g tri-coloured fusilli
1 tablespoon olive oil
1 very small red onion, finely chopped
1 large Roma (plum) tomato, roughly chopped
60 g (1/3 cup) semi-dried (sun-blushed) tomatoes, roughly chopped
2 tablespoons finely chopped coriander leaves
140 g (2/3 cup) cooked fresh or tinned crab meat
150 g Camembert cheese, rind removed, cut into small pieces
6 eggs plus 2 egg yolks

Cook the pasta in a large saucepan of boiling water until *al dente*. Drain, rinse, then drain again and set aside to cool. Meanwhile, heat half the oil in a small frying pan over low heat, add the onion and cook for 4–5 minutes, or until softened but not browned. Transfer to a bowl and add the Roma tomato, semi-dried tomatoes and coriander. Squeeze out any excess moisture from the crab meat and add the meat to the bowl. Add half the cheese to the bowl, then add the cooled pasta. Mix well. Beat together the six eggs and the two extra yolks, then stir into the tomato and crab mixture. Season.

Heat the remaining oil in the frying pan, pour in the frittata mixture and cook over low heat for 25 minutes. Preheat the grill to low. Scatter the remaining Camembert over the frittata before placing it under the grill for 10–15 minutes, or until cooked and golden brown on top. Remove from the grill and leave for 5 minutes. Cut into slices and serve with salad and some bread.

Serves 4–6

Asian tofu salad

1 large red capsicum (pepper)
1 large green capsicum (pepper)
180 g (2 cups) bean sprouts
4 spring onions, sliced diagonally
15 g (1/4 cup) chopped coriander
450 g (3 cups) shredded Chinese
 cabbage
40 g (1/4 cup) chopped roasted
 peanuts
450 g firm tofu
60 ml (1/4 cup) peanut oil

Dressing
2 tablespoons sweet chilli sauce
2 tablespoons lime juice
1/2 teaspoon sesame oil
1 1/2 tablespoons light soy sauce
1 garlic clove, finely chopped
3 teaspoons finely grated fresh ginger
60 ml (1/4 cup) peanut oil

Thinly slice the capsicums, and combine with the bean sprouts, spring onion, coriander, cabbage and peanuts.

Drain the liquid from the tofu and cut into 8 x 2 cm wide slices. Heat the oil in a large, frying pan. Cook the tofu for 2–3 minutes on each side, or until it is golden with a crispy edge, and add to the salad.

To make the dressing, mix together the chilli sauce, lime juice, oil, soy, garlic and ginger. Whisk in the peanut oil, then toss through the salad and serve immediately.

Serves 4–6

Prawn and rice noodle salad

250 g rice stick noodles
700 g medium cooked prawns, peeled and deveined, with tails intact
1 carrot, coarsely grated
1 small Lebanese cucumber, thinly sliced
30 g (1 cup) coriander leaves
80 g (½ cup) roasted unsalted peanuts, chopped
50 g (¼ cup) crisp fried shallots (see Note)

Dressing
125 ml (½ cup) rice vinegar
1 tablespoon grated palm sugar or soft brown sugar
1 garlic clove, finely chopped
2 red chillies, finely chopped
60 ml (¼ cup) fish sauce
60 ml (¼ cup) lime juice
2 tablespoons peanut oil

Soak the noodles in boiling water in a large heatproof bowl for 10 minutes. Drain, rinse under cold water to cool, and drain again. Place in a large serving bowl.

Add the prawns, carrot, cucumber and coriander to the bowl and toss.

To make the dressing, combine the vinegar, sugar and garlic in a small saucepan and bring to the boil, then reduce the heat and simmer for 3 minutes to slightly reduce the liquid. Transfer to a bowl and add the chilli, fish sauce and lime juice. Slowly whisk in the oil, and season to taste.

Toss the dressing through the salad, then scatter with the peanuts and crisp fried shallots and serve.

Serves 4

Note: Crisp fried shallots are red Asian shallot flakes used as a garnish in Southeast Asia. They are available from Asian food stores.

Chargrilled vegetable terrine

8 large slices chargrilled eggplant
(aubergine), drained
10 slices chargrilled red capsicum
(pepper), drained
8 slices chargrilled zucchini
(courgette), drained
350 g ricotta cheese
2 garlic cloves, crushed
45 g rocket
3 marinated artichokes, drained and
sliced
85 g semi-dried (sun-blushed)
tomatoes, drained and chopped
100 g marinated mushrooms, drained
and halved

Line a 23.5 x 13 x 6.5 cm loaf tin
with plastic wrap, leaving a generous
overhang on each side. Line the base
with half the eggplant, cutting to fit.
Next layer in half the capsicum, then
all of the zucchini.

Beat the ricotta and garlic together
until smooth. Season, then spread
evenly over the zucchini. Press down
firmly, and top with the rocket leaves.
Arrange the marinated artichoke,
tomato and mushrooms in three
strips over the rocket.

Top with another layer of capsicum
and finish with the eggplant. Cover
securely with the overhanging plastic
wrap. Top with a piece of cardboard
and weigh it down. Chill overnight.

Peel back the plastic wrap and
carefully turn out the terrine onto
a plate. Remove the plastic wrap
and cut into thick slices to serve.

Serves 8

Wild rice and roast chicken with Asian dressing

190 g (1 cup) wild rice
200 g (1 cup) jasmine rice
1 Chinese barbecue roast chicken
  (see Note)
15 g (¼ cup) chopped mint
15 g (¼ cup) chopped coriander
1 large Lebanese cucumber
6 spring onions
80 g (½ cup) roasted peanuts,
  roughly chopped
80 ml (⅓ cup) mirin
2 tablespoons Chinese rice wine
1 tablespoon soy sauce
1 tablespoon lime juice
2 tablespoons sweet chilli sauce,
  plus extra, to serve

Bring a large saucepan of water to the boil and add 1 teaspoon of salt and the wild rice. Cook for 30 minutes, add the jasmine rice and cook for a further 10 minutes, or until tender. Drain the rice, refresh under cold water and drain again.

Shred the chicken (the skin as well) into bite-sized pieces, place in a large bowl and add the mint and coriander. Cut the cucumber through the centre (do not peel) and slice thinly on the diagonal. Slice the spring onions on the diagonal. Add the cucumber, spring onion, rice and peanuts to the bowl with the chicken.

Mix together the mirin, rice wine, soy, lime juice and sweet chilli sauce in a small jug, pour over the salad and toss to combine. Pile the salad onto serving platters and serve with extra chilli sauce.

Serves 8

Note: It is important to use a Chinese barbecued chicken, available from Chinese barbecue shops. The flavours of five-spice and soy used to cook it will add to the flavour of the dish.

Modern salad Niçoise

60 ml (¼ cup) lemon juice
1 garlic clove, crushed
140 ml olive oil
400 g waxy potatoes, such as
    Charlotte or Kipfler
3 eggs
120 g green beans, trimmed
1 green capsicum (pepper), seeded
    and sliced
120 g black olives
300 g firm, ripe tomatoes, cut into
    wedges
100 g cucumber, cut into chunks
3 spring onions, cut into 2 cm pieces
600 g fresh tuna steaks

Place the lemon juice, garlic and 120 ml of olive oil in a jar with a screw-top lid. Season and shake the jar well to combine.

Boil the potatoes in a saucepan of salted water, for 10–12 minutes, or until tender. Add the eggs for the final 8 minutes of cooking. Drain, cool the eggs under cold water, then peel and quarter. Cool the potatoes, then cut into chunks. Bring a saucepan of salted water to the boil, add the green beans and blanch for 3 minutes. Drain and refresh under cold water. Drain well, then slice in half on the diagonal.

Place the potato and beans in a large bowl, and add the capsicum, olives, tomatoes, cucumber and spring onion. Strain the garlic from the dressing, then shake again so it is combined. Pour half over the salad, toss and transfer to a serving dish.

Heat a frying pan over very high heat. Add the remaining olive oil and allow to heat. Season the tuna steaks well on both sides and cook for 2 minutes on each side, or until rare. Allow the tuna to cool for 5 minutes, then slice thinly. Arrange on top of the salad with the eggs, and drizzle with the remaining dressing.

Serves 4

Asian pork salad

2 teaspoons rice vinegar
1 small red chilli, finely chopped
2 tablespoons light soy sauce
1 teaspoon julienned fresh ginger
1/4 teaspoon sesame oil
1 star anise
2 teaspoons lime juice
250 g Chinese roasted pork (char siu)
100 g snow pea (mangetout) sprouts
2 spring onions, thinly sliced on the
   diagonal
1/2 red capsicum (pepper), thinly sliced

For the dressing, combine the vinegar, chilli, soy sauce, ginger, sesame oil, star anise and lime juice in a small saucepan. Gently warm for 2 minutes, or until just about to come to the boil, then set aside to cool. Once it is cool, remove the star anise.

Thinly slice the pork and place in a serving bowl. Pick over the sprouts, discarding any brown or broken ones, and add to the pork. Add the spring onion and capsicum, pour on the dressing, and toss well.

Serves 4

Prawn and bean salad

200 g (1 cup) dried cannellini beans
2 red capsicums (peppers), cut into
  large flattish pieces
300 g green beans, trimmed
150 g (½ loaf) day-old ciabatta bread
  or other crusty loaf
80 ml (⅓ cup) olive oil
1 large garlic clove, finely chopped
1 kg raw medium prawns, peeled and
  deveined, with tails intact
30 g (1½ cups) flat-leaf parsley

Dressing
60 ml (¼ cup) lemon juice
60 ml (¼ cup) olive oil
2 tablespoons capers, rinsed,
  drained and chopped
1 teaspoon sugar, optional

Soak the cannellini beans in a large bowl of cold water for 8 hours. Drain then rinse the beans well, transfer to a saucepan, cover with cold water and cook for 20–30 minutes, or until tender. Drain, rinse under cold water, drain again and put in a serving bowl.

Cook the capsicum, skin-side-up, under a hot grill until the skin blackens and blisters. Cool in a plastic bag, then peel. Cut into strips, and add to the bowl.

Cook the green beans in a saucepan of boiling water for 3–4 minutes, or until tender. Drain and add to the serving bowl. Cut the bread into six slices, then cut each slice in four. Heat 60 ml (¼ cup) of the oil in a frying pan and cook the bread over medium heat on each side until golden. Remove from the pan.

Heat the remaining oil in the frying pan, add the garlic and prawns and cook for 1–2 minutes, or until the prawns are pink and cooked. Add to the salad with the parsley.

Combine the dressing ingredients, then season. Toss the dressing and bread through the salad.

Serves 4

Marinated grilled tofu salad with ginger miso dressing

80 ml (⅓ cup) tamari, shoyu or light soy sauce
2 teaspoons oil
2 garlic cloves, crushed
1 teaspoon grated fresh ginger
1 teaspoon chilli paste
500 g firm tofu, cut into 2 cm cubes
400 g mixed salad leaves
1 Lebanese cucumber, finely sliced
250 g cherry tomatoes, halved
2 teaspoons oil, extra

Dressing
2 teaspoons white miso paste
2 tablespoons mirin
1 teaspoon sesame oil
1 teaspoon grated fresh ginger
1 teaspoon finely chopped chives
1 tablespoon toasted sesame seeds

Mix together the tamari, oil, garlic, ginger, chilli paste and ½ teaspoon salt in a bowl. Add the tofu and mix until well coated. Marinate for at least 10 minutes, or preferably overnight. Drain and reserve the marinade.

To make the dressing, combine the miso with 125 ml (½ cup) hot water and leave until the miso dissolves. Add the mirin, sesame oil, ginger, chives and sesame seeds and stir thoroughly until it begins to thicken.

Combine the mesclun leaves, cucumber and tomato in a serving bowl and leave until ready to serve.

Heat the extra oil on a chargrill. Add the tofu and cook over medium heat for 4 minutes, or until golden brown. Pour on the reserved marinade and cook for 1 minute over high heat. Remove from the grill and allow to cool for 5 minutes.

Add the tofu to the salad, drizzle with the dressing and toss well.

Serves 4

Note: Miso is Japanese bean paste and plays an important part in their cuisine. It is commonly used in soups, dressings, on grilled foods and as a flavouring for pickles.

Chicken and tzatziki wrap

½ telegraph cucumber, seeded and
   grated
100 g low-fat natural yoghurt
¼ teaspoon lemon juice
1 tablespoon chopped mint
4 skinless chicken thigh fillets
pinch paprika
4 sheets lavash or other flat bread
   (see Note)
4 large butter lettuce leaves

Sprinkle the grated cucumber with
½ teaspoon salt. Leave the cucumber
for 10 minutes, then drain and mix
with the yoghurt, lemon juice and
mint. Season.

Flatten the chicken thigh fillets with
a meat mallet or rolling pin, season
and sprinkle with the paprika. Grill
the fillets for 5–7 minutes on each
side, or until cooked through.

Lay out the lavash breads and place
a large butter lettuce leaf on each.
Spread each with one quarter of the
tzatziki, then top with a sliced chicken
fillet. Roll up, folding one end closed.
Wrap in baking paper to serve.

Makes 4

Note: If you can't find lavash, use any
thin, flat bread that will roll up easily.

Pepper-crusted salmon salad

1 tablespoon coarsely ground black pepper
4 salmon fillets (approximately 180 g each), skin removed
80 g (1/3 cup) mayonnaise
1 1/2 tablespoons lemon juice
2 teaspoons creamed horseradish
1 small garlic clove, crushed
2 tablespoons chopped parsley
100 g watercress
3 tablespoons olive oil
25 g butter
100 g butter lettuce

Mix the pepper and 1/4 teaspoon salt together in a bowl, and coat both sides of each salmon fillet, pressing the pepper down firmly with your fingers. Chill for 30 minutes.

Blend the mayonnaise, lemon juice, horseradish, garlic, parsley, 60 g of the watercress, 1 tablespoon of oil and 1 tablespoon of warm water in a food processor for 1 minute. Chill.

Heat the butter and 1 tablespoon oil in a large frying pan until bubbling. Add the salmon fillets and cook over medium–high heat for 2–3 minutes each side, or until cooked to your liking. Remove from the pan and allow to cool slightly.

Wash and dry the butter lettuce, and tear into small pieces. Arrange the lettuce and remaining watercress in the centre of four serving plates, and drizzle lightly with the remaining olive oil. Break each salmon fillet into four or five pieces and arrange over the lettuce. Pour the dressing over the salmon and in a circle around the outside of the leaves.

Serves 4

Roasted tomato and pasta salad with pesto

140 ml olive oil
500 g cherry tomatoes
5 garlic cloves, unpeeled
400 g penne pasta
90 g (⅓ cup) pesto
3 tablespoons balsamic vinegar

basil leaves

Preheat the oven to 180°C (350°F/ Gas 4). Place 2 tablespoons of oil in a roasting dish and place in the hot oven for 5 minutes. Add the tomatoes and garlic to the dish, season well and toss until the tomatoes are well coated. Return to the oven and roast for 30 minutes.

Meanwhile, cook the pasta in a large saucepan of rapidly boiling water until *al dente*. Drain and transfer to a large serving bowl.

Squeeze the flesh from the roasted garlic cloves into a bowl. Add the remaining olive oil, the pesto, vinegar and 3 tablespoons of the tomato cooking juices. Season with a little salt and pepper, and toss to combine. Add to the pasta and mix well, ensuring that the pasta is coated in the dressing. Gently stir in the cherry tomatoes, then scatter with basil. This salad can be prepared up to 4 hours ahead, and served warm or cold.

Serves 4

Beef teriyaki with cucumber salad

80 ml (⅓ cup) soy sauce
2 tablespoons mirin
1 tablespoon sake (optional)
1 garlic clove, crushed
1 teaspoon grated fresh ginger
4 fillet steaks
1 teaspoon sugar
1 teaspoon toasted sesame seeds

Cucumber salad
1 large Lebanese cucumber, peeled,
 seeded and diced
½ red capsicum (pepper), diced
2 spring onions, sliced thinly on the
 diagonal
2 teaspoons sugar
1 tablespoon rice wine vinegar

Combine the soy, mirin, sake, garlic and ginger and pour over the steaks. Cover with plastic wrap and chill for at least 30 minutes.

To make the cucumber salad, place the cucumber, capsicum and spring onion in a bowl. Place the sugar, rice wine vinegar and 60 ml (¼ cup) water in a saucepan and stir over medium heat until the sugar dissolves. Increase the heat and simmer for 3–4 minutes, or until thickened. Pour over the cucumber salad, stir to combine and leave to cool completely.

Spray a chargrill plate with oil spray and heat until very hot. Drain the steaks and reserve the marinade. Cook for 3–4 minutes on each side, or until cooked to your liking. Rest the meat for 5–10 minutes.

Place the sugar and the reserved marinade in a saucepan and heat, stirring, until the sugar has dissolved. Bring to the boil and simmer for 2 minutes. Keep warm.

Slice each steak into 1 cm strips and arrange a steak on each plate. Spoon on some of the marinade, some salad and garnish with sesame seeds. Serve with steamed rice and the remaining cucumber salad.

Serves 4

Tofu kebabs with coriander miso

1 large red capsicum (pepper), cut
  into squares
12 button mushrooms, halved
6 pickling onions, quartered
3 zucchini (courgettes), cut into 3 cm
  chunks
450 g firm tofu, cut into 2 cm cubes
125 ml (½ cup) light olive oil
60 ml (¼ cup) light soy sauce
2 garlic cloves, crushed
2 teaspoons grated fresh ginger

Coriander miso
80 g (½ cup) unsalted roasted
  peanuts
60 g (2 cups) firmly packed coriander
  leaves
2 tablespoons white miso paste
2 garlic cloves
100 ml olive oil

Soak 12 wooden skewers in cold water for 10 minutes. Thread the vegetable pieces and tofu alternately onto the skewers, then place in a large rectangular ceramic dish.

Combine the olive oil, soy sauce, garlic and ginger in a bowl, then pour half the mixture over the kebabs. Cover with plastic wrap and marinate for 1 hour.

To make the miso pesto, finely chop the peanuts, coriander leaves, miso paste and garlic in a food processor. Slowly add the olive oil while the machine is still running and blend until a smooth paste.

Heat a grill plate and cook the kebabs, turning and brushing frequently with the remaining marinade, for 4–6 minutes, or until the edges are slightly brown. Serve with steamed rice and a little of the miso pesto.

Serves 4

Chilli chicken and cashew salad

3 tablespoons sweet chilli sauce
2 tablespoons lime juice
2 teaspoons fish sauce
2 tablespoons chopped coriander
1 garlic clove, crushed
1 small red chilli, finely chopped
1½ teaspoons grated fresh ginger
2 tablespoons olive oil
600 g chicken breast fillets
100 g salad leaves
250 g cherry tomatoes, halved
100 g Lebanese cucumber, cut into bite-sized chunks
50 g snow pea (mangetout) sprouts, trimmed
80 g (½ cup) cashew nuts, roughly chopped

Combine the chilli sauce, lime juice, fish sauce, coriander, garlic, chilli, ginger and 1 tablespoon of the oil in a large bowl.

Heat the remaining oil in a frying or chargrill pan over medium heat until hot, and cook the chicken for 5–8 minutes on each side or until cooked through. While still hot, slice each breast widthways into 1 cm slices and toss in the bowl with the dressing. Leave to cool slightly.

Combine the salad leaves, cherry tomatoes, cucumber chunks and snow pea sprouts in a serving bowl. Add the chicken and all of the dressing, and toss gently until the leaves are lightly coated. Scatter with chopped cashews and serve.

Serves 4

Squid salad with salsa verde

800 g small–medium squid, cleaned,
   scored and sliced into 4 cm
   diamonds
2 tablespoons olive oil
2 tablespoons lime juice
150 g green beans
150 g asparagus spears
1 teaspoon oil, extra
100 g baby rocket

Salsa verde
1 thick slice white bread, crusts
   removed
140 ml olive oil
3 tablespoons finely chopped parsley
2 teaspoons finely grated lemon zest
60 ml (¼ cup) lemon juice
2 anchovy fillets, finely chopped
2 tablespoons capers, rinsed and
   drained
1 garlic clove, crushed

Combine the squid pieces in a bowl
with the olive oil, lime juice, and a little
salt and pepper, then cover with
plastic wrap and place in the
refrigerator to marinate for 2 hours.

To make the salsa verde, break the
bread into chunks and drizzle with
2 tablespoons of oil, mixing with your
hands so that the oil is absorbed.
Place the bread and remaining oil in
a food processor with the remaining
salsa ingredients, and blend to a
paste. If it is too thick, thin with lemon
juice and olive oil, to taste.

Trim the green beans and asparagus,
and cut in half on the diagonal.
Blanch the beans for 3 minutes,
refresh under cold water, then drain.
Blanch the asparagus for 1–2 minutes,
refresh in cold water then drain.

Heat the extra oil in a frying pan over
high heat, and cook the marinated
squid in batches for 3 minutes per
batch or until cooked. Cool slightly.

Combine the green beans, asparagus,
rocket and squid. Add 3 tablespoons
of the salsa verde and toss gently.
Arrange on a serving platter and
drizzle with another tablespoon of
salsa verde.

Serves 4

Piri piri prawns

1 kg raw large prawns
4 long red chillies, deseeded
185 ml (¾ cup) white wine vinegar
2 large garlic cloves, chopped
6–8 small red chillies, chopped
125 ml (½ cup) olive oil
150 g mixed lettuce leaves

Remove the heads from the prawns. Slice the prawns down the back without cutting right through, leaving the tail intact. Open the prawn out and remove the vein. Place the prawns in a non-metallic bowl, cover and refrigerate until needed.

Place the long chillies in a saucepan with the vinegar and simmer over medium–high heat for 5 minutes, or until the chillies are soft. Cool slightly. Transfer the chillies and 60 ml (¼ cup) of the vinegar to a food processor (reserve the rest of the vinegar), then add the garlic and chopped chilli and blend until smooth.

With the motor running, gradually add the oil and remaining vinegar and process until well combined. Coat the prawns in the sauce, then cover and chill for 30 minutes.

Heat a chargrill pan or barbecue to high. Oil the pan, then cook the prawns, basting with the marinade, for 2–3 minutes each side, or until cooked. Boil the remaining marinade in a small saucepan, then reduce the heat and simmer for 3–4 minutes, or until slightly thickened and reduced. Divide the lettuce among four plates and arrange the prawns on top. Serve immediately with the remaining sauce.

Serves 4

Tofu fajitas

4 tablespoons light soy sauce
2 garlic cloves, crushed
400 g smoked tofu, cut into 5 cm
  strips
200 g tinned tomatoes
1 small onion, roughly chopped
1 small red chilli, seeded and finely
  chopped
3 tablespoons chopped coriander
  leaves
1 large ripe avocado
2 teaspoons lemon juice
250 g (1 cup) sour cream
2 tablespoons oil
1 red capsicum (pepper), seeded
  and sliced
1 yellow capsicum (pepper), seeded
  and sliced
8 spring onions, cut into 5 cm lengths
8 large (15 cm) flour tortillas

Place the soy sauce, garlic and
1 teaspoon pepper in a shallow dish.
Add the tofu and toss together well.
Cover and leave to marinate.

Combine the tomatoes, onion, chilli
and coriander in a food processor
until smooth. Season with salt and
pepper. Transfer to a small saucepan,
and bring to the boil. Reduce the heat
and simmer for 10 minutes. Cool.

Halve the avocado and remove the
stone. Scoop out the flesh and add
the lemon juice and 2 tablespoons
of the sour cream. Season and mash
well with a fork.

Heat 1 tablespoon oil in a frying pan.
Add the tofu and remaining marinade
and cook, stirring, over high heat for
4–5 minutes. Remove from the pan.
Heat the remaining oil in the pan.
Add the capsicum and spring onion,
season and cook for 3–4 minutes.

Dry-fry the tortillas over high heat for
5 seconds on each side.

To serve, spread a tortilla with a little
avocado mixture, tomato salsa and
sour cream. Top with some tofu and
vegetables, fold in one end and roll.
Repeat with the remaining tortillas
and fillings.

Serves 4

Sesame-coated tuna with coriander salsa

4 tuna steaks
115 g (3/4 cup) sesame seeds
olive oil for shallow-frying
100 g baby rocket

Coriander salsa
2 tomatoes, seeded and diced
1 large garlic clove, crushed
2 tablespoons finely chopped
   coriander leaves
2 tablespoons virgin olive oil
1 tablespoon lime juice

chilli jam, optional

Cut each tuna steak into three pieces. Place the sesame seeds on a sheet of baking paper. Roll the tuna in the sesame seeds to coat. Refrigerate for 15 minutes.

To make the salsa, place the tomato, garlic, coriander, oil and lime juice in a bowl, and mix together well. Cover and refrigerate until ready to use.

Fill a heavy-based frying pan to 1.5 cm with the oil and place over high heat. Add the tuna in two batches and cook for 2 minutes each side (it should be pink in the centre). Remove and drain on paper towels. To serve, divide the rocket among four serving plates and arrange the tuna over the top. Spoon the salsa on the side and serve immediately. Top with a teaspoon of chilli jam, if desired, and season.

Serves 4

Warm minted chicken and pasta salad

250 g cotelli pasta
125 ml (½ cup) olive oil
1 large red capsicum (pepper)
3 chicken breast fillets
6 spring onions, cut into 2 cm lengths
4 garlic cloves, thinly sliced
35 g (¾ cup) chopped mint
80 ml (⅓ cup) cider vinegar
100 g baby English spinach leaves

Cook the pasta in a large saucepan of boiling water until *al dente*, drain, stir in 1 tablespoon of the oil and set aside. Meanwhile, cut the capsicum into quarters, removing the seeds and membrane. Place, skin-side-up, under a hot grill for 8–10 minutes, or until the skin blackens and blisters. Cool in a plastic bag, then peel away the skin. Cut into thin strips. Place the chicken between two sheets of plastic wrap and press with the palm of your hand until slightly flattened.

Heat 1 tablespoon of the oil in a large frying pan, add the chicken and cook over medium heat for 2–3 minutes each side, or until light brown and cooked through. Remove from the pan and cut into 5 mm slices.

Add another tablespoon of the oil to the pan and add the spring onion, sliced garlic and capsicum and cook, stirring, for 2–3 minutes, or until starting to soften. Add 25 g (½ cup) of the mint, the vinegar and the remaining oil and stir until warmed through. In a large bowl, combine the pasta, chicken, spinach, onion mixture and remaining mint and toss well, seasoning to taste. Serve warm.

Serves 4

Pork and veal terrine

8–10 thin slices rindless streaky
  bacon
1 tablespoon olive oil
1 onion, chopped
2 garlic cloves, crushed
1 kg minced pork and veal
80 g (1 cup) fresh breadcrumbs
1 egg, beaten
60 ml (¼ cup) brandy
3 teaspoons chopped thyme
15 g (¼ cup) chopped parsley

Preheat the oven to 180°C (350°F/
Gas 4). Lightly grease a 25 x 11 cm
terrine. Line the terrine with the bacon
so that it hangs over the sides.

Heat the oil in a frying pan, add
the onion and garlic and cook for
2–3 minutes, or until the onion is
soft. Mix the onion with the mince,
breadcrumbs, egg, brandy, thyme
and parsley in a large bowl. Season.
Fry a piece of the mixture to check
the seasoning, and adjust if necessary.

Spoon the mixture into the lined
terrine, pressing down firmly. Fold
the bacon over the top, cover with
foil and place in a baking dish.

Place enough cold water in the baking
dish to come half-way up the side of
the terrine. Bake for 1–1¼ hours, or
until the juices run clear when the
terrine is pierced with a skewer.
Remove the terrine from the water-
filled baking dish and pour off the
excess juices. Cover with foil, then
put a piece of heavy cardboard,
cut to fit, on top of the terrine. Put
weights or food tins on top of the
cardboard to compress the terrine.
Refrigerate overnight, then cut into
slices to serve.

Serves 6

Roast duck salad with chilli dressing

½ teaspoon chilli flakes
2½ tablespoons fish sauce
1 tablespoon lime juice
2 teaspoons grated palm sugar
1 Chinese roasted duck
1 small red onion, thinly sliced
1 tablespoon julienned fresh ginger
20 g (⅓ cup) roughly chopped
  coriander
20 g (⅓ cup) roughly chopped mint
80 g (½ cup) roasted cashews
90 g butter lettuce

Place the chilli flakes in a frying pan and dry-fry for 30 seconds, then grind to a powder in a mortar and pestle or spice grinder. Combine the chilli with the fish sauce, lime juice and palm sugar in a bowl, and set aside.

Remove the flesh from the duck and cut it into bite-sized pieces. Place the duck in a bowl with the onion, ginger, coriander, mint and cashews. Pour in the dressing and toss gently.

Place the lettuce on a serving platter. Top with the duck salad and serve.

Serves 4–6

Seafood salad

500 g small squid
1 kg large clams
1 kg black mussels
500 g raw medium prawns, peeled,
    deveined, tails intact
5 tablespoons finely chopped flat-leaf
    parsley

Dressing
2 tablespoons lemon juice
80 ml (1/3 cup) olive oil
1 garlic clove, crushed

Gently pull apart the body and tentacles of the squid to separate. Remove the head by cutting below the eyes. Push out the beak and discard. Pull the quill from the body of the squid and discard. Under cold running water, pull away all the skin (the flaps can be used). Rinse well, then slice the squid into rings.

Scrub the clams and mussels and remove the beards. Discard any that are cracked or don't close when tapped. Rinse under running water. Fill a saucepan with 2 cm water, add the clams and mussels, cover, and boil for 4–5 minutes, or until the shells open. Remove, reserving the liquid. Discard any that do not open. Remove the mussels and clams from their shells and place in a bowl.

Bring 1 litre water to the boil and add the prawns and squid. Cook for 3–4 minutes, or until the prawns turn pink and the squid is tender. Drain and add to the clams and mussels.

To make the dressing, whisk all of the ingredients together. Season. Pour over the seafood, add 4 tablespoons of the parsley and toss to coat. Cover and refrigerate for 30–40 minutes. Sprinkle with the remaining parsley and serve with fresh bread.

Serves 4

Penne with prawns

3 Roma (plum) tomatoes
375 g penne pasta
500 g cooked medium prawns
100 g baby English spinach leaves
125 g goat's cheese, crumbled
40 g (1/4 cup) pine nuts, toasted

Garlic dressing
2 garlic cloves, crushed
60 ml (1/4 cup) extra virgin olive oil
2 teaspoons finely grated lemon zest
2 tablespoons lemon juice
1 tablespoon chopped flat-leaf
   parsley

Preheat the oven to 180°C (350°F/ Gas 4). Cut each Roma tomato lengthways into six wedges and bake on a baking tray lined with baking paper for 45 minutes, or until the wedges are just starting to dry out around the edges. Remove and cool.

Cook the penne in a large saucepan of rapidly boiling salted water for 12 minutes, or until *al dente*. Drain and cool. Transfer to a large bowl.

Meanwhile, peel the prawns, leaving the tails intact. Gently pull out the dark vein from each prawn back, starting at the head end.

Add the cooled tomato, prawns, spinach and cheese to the pasta and toss well.

For the garlic dressing, place all the ingredients in a screw-top jar, screw the lid on tightly and shake well. Pour over the salad and toss until well distributed. Sprinkle with pine nuts and serve.

Serves 4

Thai marinated octopus salad

8 baby octopus or 4 large octopus,
 cut in half (about 380 g)
250 ml (1 cup) sweet chilli sauce
2 tablespoons lime juice
1 stalk lemon grass, trimmed and
 finely chopped
2 Lebanese cucumbers
50 g butter lettuce, torn into rough
 pieces
50 g (1 cup) coriander, with stalks

Using a small knife, carefully cut between the head and tentacles of the octopus, just below the eyes. Grasp the body of the octopus and push the beak out with your finger. Cut the eyes from the head of the octopus and discard the eye section. Carefully slit through one side, avoiding the ink sac, and scrape out the gut. Rinse under running water to remove any remaining gut.

Put the octopus in a bowl and add the chilli sauce, lime juice and lemon grass. Stir until well mixed. Cover with plastic wrap and chill for at least 4 hours.

Cut the cucumbers into 6 cm lengths, scoop out the seeds and discard. Cut the cucumbers into batons.

Heat a chargrill pan until hot. Remove the octopus from the marinade, reserving the marinade, and cook for 2–3 minutes or until cooked through. Cool slightly. Arrange the lettuce and coriander around the edge of a plate, and pile the octopus in the centre.

Add the remaining marinade to the chargrill pan and heat gently for 2 minutes. Toss the cucumber through the marinade to warm, then spoon over the salad.

Serves 4

Miso yakitori chicken

3 tablespoons yellow or red miso paste
2 tablespoons sugar
60 ml (¼ cup) sake
2 tablespoons mirin
1 kg chicken thighs, boned (skin on)
1 cucumber
2 spring onions, cut into 2 cm pieces

Soak 12 long wooden bamboo skewers in cold water for at least 10 minutes. Place the miso, sugar, sake and mirin in a small saucepan over medium heat and cook, stirring well, for 2 minutes, or until the sauce is smooth and the sugar has dissolved completely.

Cut the chicken into 2.5 cm cubes. Seed the cucumber and cut into 2 cm batons. Thread the chicken, cucumber and spring onion pieces alternately onto the skewers — you should have three pieces of chicken, three pieces of cucumber and three pieces of spring onion per skewer.

Cook on a chargrill plate over high heat, turning occasionally, for 10 minutes, or until the chicken is almost cooked. Brush with the miso sauce and continue cooking, then turn and brush the other side. Repeat this process once or twice until the chicken and vegetables are cooked. Serve immediately with rice and salad.

Serves 4

Squid and scallops with herb dressing

2 oranges
8 small squid
200 g scallops, without roe
2 tablespoons oil
150 g rocket
3 ripe Roma (plum) tomatoes,
  chopped

Herb dressing
50 g (1 cup) finely chopped coriander
30 g (1 cup) finely chopped flat-leaf
  parsley
2 teaspoons ground cumin
1 teaspoon paprika
60 ml (1/4 cup) lime juice
60 ml (1/4 cup) olive oil

Remove the skin and white pith from the oranges. Use a sharp knife to cut between the membranes and divide into segments. Remove the seeds.

To clean the squid, gently pull the tentacles away from the tubes. Remove the intestines from the tentacles by cutting under the eyes, then push out the beaks. Pull the quill from the tubes. Peel off the skin under cold running water. Wash the tubes and tentacles and place in a bowl of water with 1/4 teaspoon salt and mix. Cover and chill for about 30 minutes. Drain and cut the tubes into long strips and the tentacles into pieces.

Pull any membrane, vein or hard white muscle from the scallops. Rinse and pat dry.

Heat the oil in a large deep frying pan over high heat and cook the squid in batches for 1–2 minutes, or until it turns white. Do not overcook or it will be tough. Drain on paper towels. Add the scallops to the pan and cook for 1–2 minutes each side, or until tender.

Arrange the rocket on a large platter, top with seafood, tomatoes and orange segments. Whisk the dressing ingredients together and pour over the seafood.

Serves 4

Grilled lamb pittas with fresh mint salad

1 kg lean minced lamb
60 g (1 cup) finely chopped parsley
25 g (½ cup) finely chopped mint
1 onion, finely chopped
1 garlic clove, crushed
1 egg
1 teaspoon chilli sauce
4 small wholemeal pitta pockets

Mint salad
3 small vine-ripened tomatoes
1 small red onion, finely sliced
20 g (1 cup) mint
1 tablespoon olive oil
2 tablespoons lemon juice

plain yoghurt, optional

Place the lamb, parsley, mint, onion, garlic, egg and chilli sauce in a bowl and mix together. Shape into eight small patties. Chill for 30 minutes. Preheat the oven to 160°C (315°F/ Gas 2–3).

To make the mint salad, slice the tomatoes into thin rings and place in a bowl with the onion, mint, olive oil and lemon juice. Season well with salt and pepper. Gently toss to coat.

Wrap the pitta breads in foil and warm in the oven for 5–10 minutes.

Heat a chargrill or hot plate and brush with a little oil. When very hot, cook the patties for 3 minutes on each side. Do not turn until a nice crust has formed on the base or they will fall apart.

Remove the pitta breads from the oven. Cut the pockets in half, fill each half with some mint salad and a lamb patty. Serve with some plain yoghurt, if desired.

Serves 4

Blackened chicken with crispy tortillas

4 vine-ripened tomatoes, cut into
  1 cm slices
1 teaspoon caster sugar
1 red onion, sliced
150 ml olive oil
1 ripe avocado
60 g ($\frac{1}{4}$ cup) sour cream
100 ml milk
2 tablespoons lime juice
2 x 16 cm corn tortillas
1 teaspoon dried oregano
2$\frac{1}{2}$ teaspoons ground cumin
1$\frac{1}{4}$ teaspoons garlic salt
$\frac{1}{2}$ teaspoon cayenne pepper
4 small skinless chicken breast fillets
  (about 600 g)
15 g ($\frac{1}{2}$ cup) coriander leaves

Place the tomato slices in a wide dish, sprinkle with sugar and season well. Layer the onion over the top and drizzle with 60 ml ($\frac{1}{4}$ cup) of oil. Chill for 20 minutes.

Blend the avocado, sour cream, milk, lime juice and 80 ml ($\frac{1}{3}$ cup) water in a food processor for 1 minute or until smooth. Season.

Cut each of the corn tortillas into eight 2 cm strips. Combine the oregano, cumin, garlic salt and cayenne pepper, and coat the chicken breasts in the spice mixture, pressing down firmly with your fingers. Heat 1$\frac{1}{2}$ tablespoons of oil over medium–high heat in a large, non-stick frying pan until hot. Cook the chicken breasts for 4–5 minutes on each side, or until cooked through. Cool, then refrigerate. In the same pan add 60 ml ($\frac{1}{4}$ cup) of oil. Fry the tortilla strips until golden, turning once during cooking.

On each plate arrange the tomato and onion slices in a small circle. Slice each chicken breast on the diagonal into 2 cm pieces and arrange over the tomato. Spoon the dressing over the chicken and arrange four tortilla strips over the top. Sprinkle with coriander leaves and serve immediately.

Serves 4

Salmon fillets with lemon hollandaise sauce

Lemon hollandaise sauce
175 g butter
4 egg yolks
2 tablespoons lemon juice

2 tablespoons olive oil
4 salmon fillets with skin on

Melt the butter in a small saucepan over low heat. Skim any froth from the surface and discard. Leave to cool. Whisk the yolks and 2 tablespoons water in a separate small saucepan for 30 seconds, or until pale and foamy. Place the saucepan over very low heat and whisk the egg mixture for 2–3 minutes, or until it is frothy and the whisk leaves a trail behind it as you whisk. Don't let the saucepan get too hot or you will scramble the eggs. Remove from the heat.

Add the cooled butter to the eggs, a little at a time, whisking well after each addition. Avoid using the milky whey from the base of the saucepan. Stir in the lemon juice and season with salt and cracked black pepper.

Heat the oil in a large non-stick frying pan over high heat and cook the salmon fillets skin-side-down for 2 minutes. Turn over and cook for 2 minutes, or until cooked to your liking. Serve with the sauce and vegetables of your choice.

Serves 4

Spaghetti Niçoise

350 g spaghetti
8 quail eggs (or 4 hen eggs)
1 lemon
3 x 185 g tins good-quality tuna in oil
50 g (⅓ cup) stoned and halved
  Kalamata olives
100 g semi-dried (sun-blushed)
  tomatoes, halved lengthways
4 anchovy fillets, chopped into small
  pieces
3 tablespoons baby capers, drained
3 tablespoons chopped flat-leaf
  parsley

Cook the pasta in a large saucepan of boiling water until *al dente*. Meanwhile, place the eggs in a saucepan of cold water, bring to the boil and cook for 4 minutes (10 minutes for hen eggs). Drain, cool under cold water, then peel. Cut the quail eggs into halves or the hen eggs into quarters. Finely grate the zest of the lemon to give 1 teaspoon of grated zest. Then, squeeze the lemon to give 2 tablespoons juice.

Empty the tuna and its oil into a large bowl. Add the olives, tomato halves, anchovies, lemon zest and juice, capers and 2 tablespoons of the parsley. Drain the pasta and rinse in a little cold water, then toss gently through the tuna mixture. Divide among the serving bowls, garnish with egg and the remaining chopped parsley, and serve.

Serves 4–6

Smoked chicken and pasta salad with mustard dressing

1 tablespoon balsamic vinegar
150 ml olive oil
1 tablespoon lemon juice
3 tablespoons wholegrain mustard
200 g bucatini
450 g good-quality smoked chicken
    breast
8 small radishes
2 small Fuji apples
4 spring onions, finely sliced
35 g rocket

Combine the vinegar, olive oil, lemon juice and mustard in a screw-top jar, and shake well to combine. Season to taste with salt and pepper. Bring a large saucepan of salted water to the boil, and cook the bucatini according to the packet instructions until *al dente*. Drain, rinse under cold water and drain again. Toss one-third of the dressing through the bucatini and set aside for 30 minutes.

Cut the chicken breast on the diagonal and place in a large bowl. Thinly slice the radishes and add to the chicken. Quarter, core and cube the apples without peeling them, and add to the chicken with the sliced spring onion and rocket. Pour in the remaining dressing and toss lightly.

Gently mix the pasta with the smoked chicken until well combined. Divide the salad among four serving dishes and serve with fresh, crusty bread. May be served cold as a light meal or entrée.

Serves 4

Notes: Bucatini is a thick, spaghetti-like pasta with a hollow centre. It has a chewy texture.
Smoked chicken often has a dark skin. You may wish to remove this to improve the appearance of the salad.

Prosciutto and vegetable pasta bake

3 tablespoons olive oil
35 g (1/3 cup) dried breadcrumbs
250 g pasta shapes
6 thin slices prosciutto, chopped
1 red onion, chopped
1 red capsicum (pepper), chopped
100 g (1/2 cup) semi-dried (sun-
    blushed) tomatoes,
    roughly chopped
3 tablespoons shredded basil
100 g (1 cup) grated fresh Parmesan
    cheese
4 eggs, lightly beaten
250 ml (1 cup) milk

Preheat the oven to 180°C (350°F/ Gas 4). Grease a 25 cm round ovenproof dish with a little of the olive oil and sprinkle the dish with 2 tablespoons of the breadcrumbs to coat the base and side. Cook the pasta in a large saucepan of boiling water until *al dente*. Drain and transfer to a large bowl.

Heat 1 tablespoon of the remaining oil in a large frying pan. Add the prosciutto and onion and cook over medium heat for 4–5 minutes, or until softened and golden in colour. Add the capsicum and semi-dried tomato and cook for a further 1–2 minutes. Add to the pasta with the basil and Parmesan and toss together. Spoon the mixture into the prepared dish.

Place the eggs and milk in a bowl, whisk together, then season with salt and pepper. Pour the egg mixture over the pasta. Season the remaining breadcrumbs, add the remaining oil and toss together. Sprinkle the seasoned breadcrumb mixture over the pasta. Bake for 40 minutes, or until set. Allow to stand for 5 minutes, then cut into wedges and serve with a green salad, if desired.

Serves 6–8

Tuna and white bean salad

400 g tuna steaks
1 small red onion, thinly sliced
1 tomato, seeded and chopped
1 small red capsicum (pepper), thinly
  sliced
2 x 400 g tins cannellini beans
2 garlic cloves, crushed
1 teaspoon chopped thyme
4 tablespoons finely chopped flat-leaf
  parsley
1½ tablespoons lemon juice
80 ml (⅓ cup) extra virgin olive oil
1 teaspoon honey
olive oil, for brushing
100 g rocket
1 teaspoon lemon zest

Place the tuna steaks on a plate, sprinkle with cracked black pepper on both sides, cover with plastic and refrigerate until needed.

Combine the onion, tomato and capsicum in a large bowl. Rinse the cannellini beans under cold running water for 30 seconds, drain and add to the bowl with the garlic, thyme and 3 tablespoons of the parsley.

Place the lemon juice, oil and honey in a small saucepan, bring to the boil, then simmer, stirring, for 1 minute, or until the honey dissolves. Remove from the heat.

Brush a barbecue or chargrill with olive oil, and heat until very hot. Cook the tuna for 1 minute on each side. The meat should still be pink in the middle. Slice into 3 cm cubes and combine with the salad. Pour on the warm dressing and toss well.

Place the rocket on a platter. Top with the salad, season and garnish with the zest and remaining parsley.

Serves 4–6

Thai noodle salad

Dressing
2 tablespoons grated fresh ginger
2 tablespoons soy sauce
2 tablespoons sesame oil
80 ml (1/3 cup) red wine vinegar
1 tablespoon sweet chilli sauce
2 garlic cloves, crushed
80 ml (1/3 cup) kecap manis

500 g cooked large prawns
250 g dried instant egg noodles
5 spring onions, sliced diagonally
2 tablespoons chopped coriander
1 red capsicum (pepper), diced
100 g snow peas (mangetout), sliced

For the dressing, whisk together the fresh ginger, soy sauce, sesame oil, red wine vinegar, chilli sauce, garlic and kecap manis in a large bowl.

Peel the prawns and gently pull out the dark vein from each prawn back, starting at the head end. Cut each prawn in half lengthways.

Cook the egg noodles in a saucepan of boiling water for 2 minutes, or until tender, then drain thoroughly. Cool in a large bowl.

Add the dressing, prawns and remaining ingredients to the noodles and toss gently. Can be served with lime wedges.

Serves 4

Prawn and fennel salad

1.25 kg raw large prawns, peeled and
  deveined
1 large fennel bulb, thinly sliced
  (400 g)
300 g watercress
2 tablespoons finely chopped chives
125 ml (½ cup) extra virgin olive oil
60 ml (¼ cup) lemon juice
1 tablespoon Dijon mustard
1 large garlic clove, finely chopped

Bring a saucepan of water to the boil, then add the prawns, return to the boil and simmer for 2 minutes, or until the prawns turn pink and are cooked through. Drain and leave to cool. Pat the prawns dry with paper towels and slice in half lengthways. Place in a large serving bowl.

Add the fennel, watercress and chives to the bowl and mix well.

To make the dressing, whisk the oil, lemon juice, mustard and garlic together until combined. Pour the dressing over the salad, season with salt and cracked black pepper and toss gently. Arrange the salad on serving plates and serve immediately.

Serves 4

Somen noodle salad with sesame dressing

Sesame dressing
40 g (1/3 cup) sesame seeds, toasted
2 1/2 tablespoons shoyu or light
  soy sauce
2 tablespoons rice vinegar
2 teaspoons sugar
1/2 teaspoon grated fresh ginger
1/2 teaspoon dashi granules

125 g dried somen noodles
100 g snow peas (mangetout), finely
  sliced on the diagonal
100 g daikon radish, julienned
100 g (1 small) carrot, julienned
1 spring onion, sliced on the diagonal
50 g baby English spinach leaves,
  trimmed
2 teaspoons toasted sesame seeds

To make the dressing, place the sesame seeds in a mortar and pestle and grind until fine and moist. Combine the soy sauce, rice vinegar, sugar, ginger, dashi granules and 125 ml (1/2 cup) water in a small saucepan and bring to the boil over high heat. Reduce the heat to medium and simmer, stirring, for 2 minutes, or until the dashi granules have dissolved. Remove from the heat. Cool. Gradually combine with the ground sesame seeds, stirring to form a thick dressing.

Cook the noodles in a large saucepan of boiling water for 2 minutes, or until tender. Drain, rinse under cold water and cool completely. Cut into 10 cm lengths using scissors.

Place the snow peas in a large shallow bowl with the daikon, carrot, spring onion, English spinach leaves and the noodles. Add the dressing and toss well to combine. Place in the refrigerator until ready to serve. Just before serving, sprinkle the top with the toasted sesame seeds.

Serves 4

Barbecued tuna and Mediterranean vegetables

185 ml (³/₄ cup) olive oil
3 garlic cloves, crushed
2 tablespoons sweet chilli sauce
1 red capsicum (pepper), cut into
  3 cm pieces
1 yellow capsicum (pepper), cut into
  3 cm pieces
2 large zucchini (courgettes), cut into
  1.5 cm slices
2 long, thin eggplants (aubergines),
  cut into 1.5 cm slices
olive oil, extra, for brushing
4 tuna steaks

Lemon and caper mayonnaise
1 egg yolk
1 teaspoon grated lemon zest
2 tablespoons lemon juice
1 small garlic clove, chopped
185 ml (³/₄ cup) olive oil
1 tablespoon baby capers, rinsed
  and drained

Combine the olive oil, garlic and sweet chilli sauce. Add the capsicum, zucchini and eggplant, toss well, then marinate for 30 minutes.

For the mayonnaise, process the egg yolk, zest, lemon juice and garlic in a food processor or blender until smooth. With the motor running, gradually add the oil in a thin steady stream until the mixture thickens and is a creamy consistency. Stir in the capers and ¹/₂ teaspoon salt.

Heat the barbecue or a chargrill plate, brush with oil and cook the drained vegetables for 4–5 minutes each side, or until cooked through. Keep warm.

Brush the tuna steaks with extra oil and barbecue for 2–3 minutes each side, or until just cooked (tuna should be rare in the centre). Arrange the vegetables and tuna steaks on serving plates and serve with the lemon and caper mayonnaise.

Serves 4

Stracci with artichokes and chargrilled chicken

1 tablespoon olive oil
3 chicken breast fillets
500 g stracci pasta
8 slices prosciutto
280 g jar artichokes in oil, drained and
  quartered, oil reserved
150 g semi-dried (sunblushed)
  tomatoes, thinly sliced
80 g baby rocket
2–3 tablespoons balsamic vinegar

Lightly brush a chargrill or frying pan with the oil and heat over high heat. Cook the chicken for 6–8 minutes each side, or until cooked through. Cut into thin slices on the diagonal.

Cook the pasta in a large saucepan of boiling water until *al dente*.

Meanwhile, place the prosciutto on a lined grill tray and cook under a hot grill for 2 minutes each side, or until crisp. Cool slightly and break into pieces. Drain the pasta, then combine with the chicken, prosciutto, artichokes, tomato and rocket in a bowl and toss. Whisk together 60 ml (1/4 cup) of the reserved artichoke oil and the balsamic vinegar and toss through the pasta mixture. Season to taste with salt and cracked black pepper, then serve.

Serves 6

Goat's cheese tart

Pastry
125 g (1 cup) plain flour
60 ml (¼ cup) olive oil

Filling
1 tablespoon olive oil
2 onions, thinly sliced
1 teaspoon thyme leaves
125 g ricotta cheese
100 g goat's cheese
2 tablespoons pitted Niçoise olives
1 egg, lightly beaten
60 ml (¼ cup) cream

For the pastry, sift the flour and a pinch of salt into a large bowl and make a well. Add the olive oil and mix with a flat-bladed knife until crumbly. Gradually add 3–4 tablespoons cold water until the mixture comes together. Remove and pat together to form a disc. Chill for 30 minutes.

For the filling, heat the olive oil in a frying pan. Add the onion, cover and cook over low heat for 30 minutes. Season and stir in half the thyme. Cool slightly.

Preheat the oven to 180° C (350°F/ Gas 4). Lightly flour the work bench and roll out the pastry to a 30 cm circle. Evenly spread the onion over the pastry, leaving a 2 cm border. Sprinkle the ricotta and the goat's cheese evenly over the onion. Place the olives over the cheeses, then sprinkle with the remaining thyme. Fold the pastry border in to the edge of the filling, gently pleating as you go.

Combine the egg and cream, then carefully pour over the filling. Bake on a heated baking tray on the lower half of the oven for 45 minutes, or until the pastry is golden. Serve warm or at room temperature.

Serves 6

Chermoula prawns

Chermoula
80 ml (1/3 cup) virgin olive oil
3 tablespoons chopped coriander
  leaves
2 tablespoons chopped flat-leaf
  parsley
2 tablespoons chopped preserved
  lemon rind
2 tablespoons lemon juice
2 garlic cloves, chopped
1 small red chilli, seeded and finely
  chopped
1 teaspoon ground cumin
1/2 teaspoon paprika

20 raw medium prawns
370 g (2 cups) instant couscous
375 ml (1 1/2 cups) boiling chicken
  stock
1 tablespoon olive oil
2 tablespoons shredded mint leaves

Process the chermoula ingredients to a coarse purée, then season with salt.

Peel and devein the prawns, keeping the tails intact. Thread a cocktail stick through the body of each prawn to keep them straight, then place them in a dish and spoon the chermoula over them, turning to coat. Chill the prawns, covered, for 30 minutes, turning occasionally.

Place the couscous in a heatproof bowl, pour on the boiling stock and oil, cover and leave for 3–4 minutes. Fluff the couscous with a fork and stir in the mint.

Arrange the prawns on a foil-lined grill tray and cook under a hot grill for 2–3 minutes each side, or until pink and cooked. Divide the couscous and prawns among four plates.

Serves 4

Pan bagnat

4 crusty bread rolls, or 1 baguette
  sliced into 4 chunks
1 garlic clove
60 ml (1/4 cup) olive oil
1 tablespoon red wine vinegar
3 tablespoons basil leaves, torn
2 tomatoes, sliced
2 hard-boiled eggs, sliced
75 g tin tuna
8 anchovy fillets
1 small cucumber, sliced
1/2 green capsicum (pepper), thinly
  sliced
1 French shallot, thinly sliced

Slice the bread rolls in half and remove some of the soft centre from the tops. Cut the garlic clove in half and rub the insides of the rolls with the cut sides. Sprinkle both sides of the bread with olive oil, vinegar, salt and pepper.

Place all the salad ingredients on the base of the rolls, cover with the other half and wrap each sandwich in foil. Press firmly with a light weight, such as a tin of food, and leave in a cool place for 1 hour before serving.

Serves 4

Salmon with miso and soy noodles

300 g soba noodles
1 tablespoon soy bean oil
3 teaspoons white miso paste
100 ml honey
1½ tablespoons sesame oil
6 salmon fillets, boned and skin
  removed
1 teaspoon chopped garlic
1 tablespoon grated fresh ginger
1 carrot, julienned
6 small spring onions, thinly sliced
70 g (1 cup) soya bean sprouts
80 ml (⅓ cup) rice vinegar
3 tablespoons light soy sauce
1 teaspoon sesame oil, extra
1 tablespoon toasted sesame seeds

mustard cress

Preheat the oven to 180°C (350°F/ Gas 4). Fill a large saucepan three-quarters full with water and bring to the boil. Add the soba noodles and return to the boil. Cook for 1 minute, then add 250 ml (1 cup) cold water. Boil for 1–2 minutes, then add another 250 ml (1 cup) water. Boil for 2 minutes, or until tender, then drain and toss with ½ teaspoon of the soy bean oil.

Combine the miso, honey, sesame oil and 1 tablespoon water to form a paste. Brush over the salmon, then sear on a hot chargrill for 30 seconds on each side. Brush the salmon with the remaining paste and place on a baking tray. Bake for 6 minutes, then cover and rest in a warm place.

Heat the remaining soy oil in a wok. Add the garlic, ginger, carrot, spring onion and sprouts, and stir-fry for 1 minute — the vegetables should not brown, but remain crisp and bright. Add the noodles, rice vinegar, soy sauce and extra sesame oil and stir-fry quickly to heat through.

Divide the noodles among six serving plates and top with a portion of salmon and sprinkle with the sesame seeds. Garnish with the mustard cress and serve.

Serves 6

Sides

Greek salad

4 tomatoes, cut into wedges
1 telegraph cucumber, peeled,
   halved, seeded and cut into small
   cubes
2 green capsicums (peppers),
   seeded, halved lengthways and
   cut into strips
1 red onion, finely sliced
16 Kalamata olives
250 g firm feta cheese, cut into cubes
3 tablespoons flat-leaf parsley
12 whole mint leaves
125 ml (½ cup) olive oil
2 tablespoons lemon juice
1 garlic clove, crushed

Place the tomato wedges, cucumber, capsicum strips, onion, Kalamata olives, feta and half of the parsley and mint leaves in a large serving bowl, and toss together gently.

Place the oil, lemon juice and garlic in a screw-top jar, season, and shake until well combined. Pour the dressing over the salad and toss. Garnish with the remaining parsley and mint.

Serves 4

Tuscan bread salad

200 g ciabatta bread
8 vine-ripened tomatoes
80 ml (⅓ cup) olive oil
1 tablespoon lemon juice
1½ tablespoons red wine vinegar
6 anchovy fillets, finely chopped
1 tablespoon baby capers, rinsed,
   drained and finely chopped
1 garlic clove, crushed
30 g (1 cup) basil leaves

Preheat the oven to 220°C (425°F/ Gas 7). Tear the bread into 2 cm pieces, spread on a baking tray and bake for 5–7 minutes, or until golden on the outside. Leave the toasted bread on a cake rack to cool.

Score a cross in the base of each tomato. Place in a heatproof bowl and cover with boiling water. Leave for 30 seconds then transfer to cold water and peel the skin away from the cross. Cut four of the tomatoes in half and squeeze the juice and seeds into a bowl, reserving and chopping the flesh. Add the oil, juice, vinegar, anchovies, capers and garlic to the tomato juice, and season.

Seed and slice the remaining tomatoes, and place in a large bowl with the reserved tomato and most of the basil. Add the dressing and toasted bread, and toss. Garnish with the remaining basil, season, and leave for at least 15 minutes. Serve at room temperature.

Serves 6

Chargrilled vegetable salad with balsamic dressing

4 baby eggplants (aubergines)
5 Roma (plum) tomatoes
2 red capsicums (peppers)
1 green capsicum (pepper)
2 zucchini (courgettes)
100 ml olive oil
12 bocconcini or small, fresh
  mozarella
45 g (½ cup) Ligurian olives
1 garlic clove, finely chopped
3 teaspoons baby capers, rinsed
  and drained
½ teaspoon sugar
2 tablespoons balsamic vinegar

Cut the eggplant and tomatoes in half lengthways. Cut the red and green capsicums in half lengthways, remove the seeds and membrane then cut each half into three pieces. Thinly slice the zucchini on the diagonal.

Preheat a chargrill pan to hot. Add 1 tablespoon of oil and cook a quarter of the vegetables (cook the tomatoes cut-side down first) for 2–3 minutes, or until marked and golden. Place in a large bowl.

Cook the remaining vegetables in batches until tender, adding more oil as needed. Transfer to the bowl and add the baby bocconcini. Mix the olives, garlic, capers, sugar, vinegar and remaining oil (about 2 tablespoons). Pour over the salad and toss. Season with pepper.

Serves 4–6

Green salad with lemon vinaigrette

150 g baby cos lettuce
150 g small butter lettuce
50 g watercress
100 g rocket
1 tablespoon finely chopped French
  shallots
2 teaspoons Dijon mustard
1/2 teaspoon sugar
1 tablespoon finely chopped basil
1 teaspoon grated lemon zest
3 teaspoons lemon juice
1 tablespoon white wine vinegar
25 ml lemon oil
75 ml virgin olive oil

Remove the outer leaves from the cos and butter lettuces and separate the core leaves. Wash in cold water, place in a colander to drain, then refrigerate. Pinch or trim the stalks from the watercress and rocket, pat dry in a tea towel and chill with the lettuce.

To make the dressing, whisk together the shallots, mustard, sugar, basil, lemon zest, lemon juice and vinegar in a bowl until well blended. Place the oils in a small jug and slowly add to the bowl in a thin stream, whisking constantly to create a smooth, creamy dressing. Season to taste with salt and pepper.

Place the salad greens in a large bowl. Drizzle the dressing over the salad and toss gently to coat.

Serves 6

Mushroom and goat's cheese salad

Dressing
2 tablespoons lemon juice
3 tablespoons olive oil
1 teaspoon grated lemon zest

8 large cap mushrooms, stems removed
1 tablespoon chopped thyme
4 garlic cloves, finely chopped
2 tablespoons olive oil
50 g (4 cups) baby rocket
100 g goat's cheese
2 tablespoons chopped flat-leaf parsley

Preheat the oven to 200°C (400°F/ Gas 6). For the dressing, combine the juice, oil and zest in a small bowl.

Place the mushrooms on a large baking tray, sprinkle with thyme and garlic, then drizzle with olive oil. Cover with foil and roast for 20 minutes. Remove the mushrooms from the oven and toss to combine the flavours. Re-cover and roast for a further 10 minutes or until cooked. Remove the mushrooms from the oven and cut in half.

Place the rocket on a serving platter, top with the mushrooms and crumble the goat's cheese over the top. Whisk the dressing to ensure it is well combined and drizzle over the salad. Serve sprinkled with parsley.

Serves 4–6

Roasted tomato and bocconcini salad

8 Roma (plum) tomatoes, halved
pinch of sugar
125 ml (½ cup) olive oil
15 g (¼ cup) torn basil
2 tablespoons balsamic vinegar
350 g cherry bocconcini or baby
  fresh mozarella
160 g mizuna lettuce

sea salt

Preheat the oven to 150°C (300°F/ Gas 2). Place the tomato, cut-side-up, on a rack over a baking tray lined with baking paper. Sprinkle with salt, cracked black pepper, and a pinch of sugar. Roast for 2 hours, then remove from the oven and allow to cool.

Combine the oil and basil in a saucepan, and stir gently over medium heat for 3–5 minutes, or until it is very hot, but not smoking. Remove from the heat and discard the basil. Mix 2 tablespoons of oil with the vinegar.

Toss together the tomato, bocconcini and lettuce. Arrange the salad in a shallow serving bowl and drizzle with the dressing. Sprinkle with sea salt and cracked black pepper.

Serves 6

Notes: If cherry bocconcini are unavailable, use regular bocconcini cut into quarters.
Leftover basil oil can be stored in a clean jar in the refrigerator, and is great in pasta sauces.

Caramelised onion and potato salad

oil, for cooking
6 red onions, thinly sliced
1 kg Kipfler or new potatoes,
    unpeeled
4 rashers streaky bacon, rind
    removed
30 g (^{2}/$_3$ cup) chives, snipped

Mayonnaise
250 g (1 cup) whole-egg mayonnaise
1 tablespoon Dijon mustard
juice of 1 lemon
2 tablespoons sour cream

Heat 2 tablespoons of oil in a large heavy-based frying pan, add the onion and cook over medium–low heat for 40 minutes, or until soft and caramelised.

Cut the potatoes into large chunks (if they are small leave them whole). Cook in boiling water for 10 minutes, or until just tender, then drain and cool slightly. (Do not overcook the potatoes or they will fall apart.)

Grill the bacon until crisp, drain on paper towels and cool slightly before coarsely chopping.

Put the potato, onion and chives in a large bowl, reserving a few chives for a garnish, and mix well.

To make the mayonnaise, put the whole-egg mayonnaise, mustard, lemon juice and sour cream in a bowl and whisk to combine. Pour over the salad and toss to coat. Sprinkle with the bacon and garnish with the reserved chives.

Serves 10

Spinach salad with bacon and quail eggs

12 quail eggs
2 teaspoons oil
4 rashers good-quality back bacon, cut into thin strips
300 g baby English spinach leaves
200 g cherry tomatoes, halved
100 g (2/3 cup) pine nuts, toasted

Dressing
60 ml (1/4 cup) apple cider vinegar
3 garlic cloves, crushed
2 teaspoons Dijon mustard
2 teaspoons maple syrup
1 teaspoon Worcestershire sauce
60 ml (1/4 cup) olive oil

Bring a small saucepan of water to the boil, gently add the quail eggs and simmer for 1 1/2 minutes. Drain, then refresh under cold running water until cool, and peel the eggs.

Heat the oil in a non-stick frying pan over medium heat, add the bacon and cook for 5–6 minutes, or until crisp. Drain on paper towels, retaining the drippings in the pan.

Wash the spinach in cold water and remove the stems. Wrap the leaves loosely in a clean tea towel to remove any excess water. Place in a salad bowl, tearing the larger leaves if necessary, then add the tomatoes, bacon and pine nuts. Halve the eggs and scatter over the salad.

Reheat the bacon fat over medium heat, then add the vinegar, garlic, mustard, maple syrup and Worcestershire sauce. Shake the pan over the heat, for 2 minutes, or until bubbling, then add the oil and heat for another minute. Pour the warm dressing over the salad, season to taste and serve.

Serves 4–6

Tabbouleh

175 g (1 cup) burghul (bulgar)
200 g flat-leaf parsley, or 100 g
   parsley and 100 g rocket
80 g mint
6 spring onions, finely sliced
2 tomatoes, finely chopped
2 large garlic cloves, finely chopped
80 ml (1/3 cup) lemon juice
125 ml (1/2 cup) extra virgin olive oil

Place the burghul in a large bowl and add enough hot water to cover. Leave to soak for 15–20 minutes or until tender. Drain well.

Finely chop the parsley and mint, and combine in a large bowl with the drained burghul, spring onion and chopped tomato.

Mix the garlic and lemon juice together in a small jug. Whisk in the oil until it is well combined, and season to taste with salt and black pepper. Toss the dressing through the salad before serving.

Serves 6–8

Variation: Add 40 g (1/4 cup) toasted pine nuts with the burghul.

Fresh beetroot and goat's cheese salad

1 kg (4 bulbs with leaves) fresh
  beetroot
200 g green beans
1 tablespoon red wine vinegar
2 tablespoons extra virgin olive oil
1 garlic clove, crushed
1 tablespoon capers in brine, rinsed,
  drained and coarsely chopped
100 g goat's cheese

Trim the leaves from the beetroot. Scrub the bulbs and wash the leaves well. Bring a large saucepan of water to the boil, add the beetroot, then reduce the heat and simmer, covered, for 30 minutes, or until tender when pierced with the point of a knife. (The cooking time may vary depending on the size of the bulbs.) Drain and cool. Peel the skins off the beetroot and cut the bulbs into wedges.

Meanwhile, bring a saucepan of water to the boil, add the beans and cook for 3 minutes, or until just tender. Remove with tongs and plunge into a bowl of cold water. Drain well. Add the beetroot leaves to the boiling water and cook for 3–5 minutes, or until the leaves and stems are tender. Drain, plunge into a bowl of cold water, then drain again well.

To make the dressing, put the vinegar, oil, garlic, capers, 1/2 teaspoon salt and 1/2 teaspoon cracked black pepper in a jar and shake well. Divide the beans and beetroot wedges and leaves among four plates. Crumble the goat's cheese over the top and drizzle with the dressing.

Serves 4

Watercress, feta and watermelon salad

2 tablespoons sunflower seeds
475 g rindless watermelon, cut into
  1 cm cubes
180 g feta cheese, cut into 1 cm
  cubes
75 g (2½ cups) watercress sprigs
2 tablespoons olive oil
1 tablespoon lemon juice
2 teaspoons chopped oregano

Heat a small frying pan over high heat. Add the sunflower seeds and, shaking the pan continuously, dry-fry for 2 minutes, or until they are toasted and lightly golden.

Place the watermelon, feta and watercress leaves in a large serving dish and toss gently to combine. Combine the olive oil, lemon juice and chopped oregano in a small jug, and season to taste with a little salt and freshly ground black pepper (don't add too much salt as the feta is already quite salty). Pour the dressing over the salad and toss together well. Scatter with the toasted sunflower seeds, and serve.

Serves 4

Pear and walnut salad with lime vinaigrette

1 small baguette, cut into 16 thin
    slices
oil, for brushing
1 garlic clove, cut in half
100 g (1 cup) walnuts
200 g ricotta cheese
400 g mixed salad leaves
2 pears, cut into 2 cm cubes, mixed
    with 2 tablespoons lime juice

Lime vinaigrette
60 ml (¼ cup) lime juice
3 tablespoons oil
2 tablespoons raspberry vinegar

Preheat the oven to 180°C (350°F/ Gas 4). Brush the baguette slices with a little oil, rub with the cut side of the garlic, then place on a baking tray. Bake for 10 minutes, or until crisp and golden. Place the walnuts on a baking tray and roast for 5–8 minutes, or until slightly browned — shake the tray to ensure even colouring. Allow to cool for 5 minutes.

To make the lime vinaigrette, whisk together the lime juice, oil, vinegar, 1 teaspoon salt and ½ teaspoon freshly ground black pepper in a small bowl. Set aside until ready to use.

Spread some of the ricotta cheese on each crouton, then cook under a hot grill for 2–3 minutes, or until hot.

Place the mixed salad, pears and walnuts in a bowl, add the vinaigrette and toss through. Divide the salad among four serving bowls and serve with the ricotta cheese croutons.

Serves 4

Broad bean, mint and bacon salad

600 g frozen broad beans (see Notes)
150 g shredded butter or cos lettuce
35 g ($^3/_4$ cup) shredded mint
250 g Kasseler or pancetta
1 tablespoon olive oil
1$^1/_2$ teaspoons Dijon mustard
1 teaspoon sugar
2 tablespoons white wine vinegar
60 ml ($^1/_4$ cup) extra virgin olive oil
4 flatbreads to serve (eg pitta breads)

Blanch the beans, according to packet instructions. Drain, rinse under cold water, and peel. Place in a large bowl with the lettuce and mint.

Slice the Kasseler into thick slices, then into 2 cm chunks. Heat the oil in a heavy-based frying pan and cook the Kasseler for 3–4 minutes, or until golden. Add to the bean mixture.

Combine the mustard, sugar and vinegar in a jug. Whisk in the extra virgin oil until well combined and season with salt and freshly ground black pepper. Pile the salad onto fresh or lightly toasted flatbread to serve.

Serves 4

Notes: If they are in season, you may like to use fresh broad beans. You will need about 1.8 kg of beans in the pod to give 600 g of beans. Boil the beans for 2 minutes and peel before using them.
Kasseler is a traditional German speciality. It is a cured and smoked loin of pork that comes in a single piece and should be available at good delicatessens.

Radicchio with figs and ginger vinaigrette

1 radicchio
1 small curly endive lettuce (see Note)
3 oranges
1/2 small red onion, thinly sliced into rings
8 small green figs, quartered
3 tablespoons extra virgin olive oil
1 teaspoon red wine vinegar
1/8 teaspoon ground cinnamon
2 tablespoons orange juice
2 tablespoons very finely chopped glacé ginger with syrup
2 pomegranates, optional

Wash the radicchio and curly endive leaves in cold water, and drain well. Tear any large leaves into pieces.

Peel and segment the oranges, discarding all of the pith. Place in a large bowl with the onion rings, salad leaves and figs, reserving 8 fig quarters.

Combine the olive oil, vinegar, cinnamon, orange juice and ginger in a small jug. Season to taste with salt and pepper. Pour over the salad and toss lightly.

Arrange the reserved figs in pairs over the salad. If you are using the pomegranates, slice them in half and scoop out the seeds with a spoon. Scatter these over the salad before serving.

Serves 4

Note: Curly endive is also known as frisée lettuce.
Variation: A delicious alternative for this salad is to replace the oranges and orange juice with mandarins and mandarin juice when in season.

Egg salad with creamy dressing

10 large eggs, at room temperature
1 egg yolk
3 teaspoons lemon juice
2 teaspoons Dijon mustard
70 ml olive oil
70 ml oil
2 tablespoons chopped dill
30 ml crème frâiche or sour cream
2 tablespoons baby capers, rinsed
  and drained
20 g (⅓ cup) mustard cress

Place the eggs in a large saucepan of cold water. Bring to the boil and simmer gently for 10 minutes. Drain, then cool the eggs under cold running water. Remove the shells.

Place the egg yolk, lemon juice and Dijon mustard in a food processor or blender and season with salt and freshly ground black pepper. With the motor running, slowly add the combined olive oil and safflower oil, drop by drop at first, then slowly increasing the amount to a thin, steady stream as the mixture thickens. When all of the oil has been added, place the mayonnaise in a large bowl, and gently stir in the dill, crème frâiche and capers.

Roughly chop the eggs and fold into the mayonnaise. Transfer the salad to a serving bowl and use scissors to cut the green tips from the mustard cress. Scatter them over the salad and serve.

Serves 4

Serving suggestion: Serve the salad on slices of toasted bruschetta, draped with smoked salmon and topped with the mustard cress and extra black pepper.

Moroccan eggplant with couscous

185 g (1 cup) instant couscous
200 ml olive oil
1 onion, halved and sliced
1 eggplant (aubergine)
3 teaspoons ground cumin
1 1/2 teaspoons garlic salt
1/4 teaspoon ground cinnamon
1 teaspoon paprika
1/4 teaspoon ground cloves
50 g butter
30 g (1/2 cup) roughly chopped parsley

Place the couscous in a large bowl and add 375 ml (1 1/2 cups) boiling water. Leave for 10 minutes, then fluff up with a fork.

Add 2 tablespoons of oil to a large frying pan and cook the onion for 8–10 minutes, or until browned. Remove from the pan, retaining the remaining oil.

Cut the eggplant into 1 cm slices, then into quarters and place in a large bowl. Combine the cumin, garlic salt, cinnamon, paprika, cloves and 1/2 teaspoon salt, and sprinkle over the eggplant, tossing until it is well coated. Add the remaining oil to the pan and reheat over medium heat. Cook the eggplant, turning once, for 20–25 minutes, or until browned. Remove from the pan and cool.

Using the same pan, melt the butter, then add the couscous and cook for 2–3 minutes. Stir in the onion, eggplant and parsley, allow to cool, then serve.

Serves 4

Lentil salad

½ brown onion
2 cloves
300 g (1²/₃ cups) puy lentils (see Note)
1 strip lemon zest
2 garlic cloves, peeled
1 fresh bay leaf
2 teaspoons ground cumin
2 tablespoons red wine vinegar
60 ml (¼ cup) olive oil
1 tablespoon lemon juice
2 tablespoon mint leaves, finely
  chopped
3 spring onions, finely chopped

Stud the onion with the cloves and place in a saucepan with the lentils, zest, garlic, bay leaf, 1 teaspoon cumin and 875 ml (3½ cups) water. Bring to the boil and cook over medium heat for 25–30 minutes, or until the water has been absorbed. Discard the onion, zest and bay leaf. Reserve the garlic and finely chop.

Whisk together the vinegar, oil, juice, garlic and remaining cumin. Stir through the lentils with the mint and spring onion. Season well. Leave for 30 minutes to let the flavours absorb. Serve at room temperature.

Serves 4–6

Note: Puy lentils are small, green lentils from France. They are available dried from gourmet food stores.

Coleslaw

½ green cabbage
¼ red cabbage
3 carrots, coarsely grated
6 radishes, coarsely grated
1 red capsicum (pepper), chopped
4 spring onions, sliced
15 g (¼ cup) chopped parsley
250 g (1 cup) whole egg mayonnaise

Remove the hard core from the cabbages and shred the leaves with a sharp knife. Place in a large bowl and add the grated carrot, grated radish, red capsicum, spring onion and parsley to the bowl.

Add the mayonnaise, season to taste with salt and freshly ground black pepper and toss until well combined.

Serves 8–10

Note: Cover and refrigerate the chopped vegetables for up to 3 hours before serving. Add the mayonnaise just before serving.

Soba noodle salad with tahini dressing

200 g snake beans or green beans
200 g dry soba noodles
1 tablespoon tahini
1 small garlic clove, crushed
1½ tablespoons rice vinegar
1½ tablespoons olive oil
½ teaspoon sesame oil
1 teaspoon soy sauce
2 teaspoons sugar
2 spring onions, finely sliced
3 teaspoons black sesame seeds

Trim the beans, and cut into long strips on the diagonal. Place in a saucepan of boiling water and return to the boil for 2 minutes, or until tender. Drain and refresh under cold running water. Drain.

Cook the noodles in boiling water for 3–4 minutes, or until they are tender. Drain and refresh under cold water, then drain again.

Combine the tahini, crushed garlic, rice vinegar, olive oil, sesame oil, soy sauce, sugar and 2 teaspoons warm water in a screw-top jar. Shake well and season to taste.

Combine the beans, noodles, spring onion and sesame seeds in a serving bowl, add the dressing and toss lightly to combine. Serve immediately.

Serves 4–6

Note: Add the dressing as close to serving as possible, as it will be absorbed by the noodles.

Insalata Caprese

3 large vine-ripened tomatoes
250 g bocconcini (see Note)
12 basil leaves
60 ml (¼ cup) extra virgin olive oil
4 basil leaves, roughly torn, extra,
   optional

Slice the tomatoes into 1 cm slices, to make twelve slices altogether. Slice the bocconcini into twenty-four 1 cm slices.

Arrange the tomato slices on a serving plate, alternating them with two slices of bocconcini. Place the basil leaves between the bocconcini slices.

Drizzle with the oil, sprinkle with the basil, if desired, and season well with salt and ground black pepper.

Serves 4

Note: This popular salad is most successful with very fresh buffalo mozzarella if you can find it. We've used bocconcini in this recipe. These are small balls of fresh cow's milk mozzarella.

Moroccan spiced carrot salad

4 large carrots
2 cardamom pods
1 teaspoon black mustard seeds
1/2 teaspoon ground cumin
1/2 teaspoon ground ginger
1 teaspoon paprika
1/2 teaspoon ground coriander
80 ml (1/3 cup) olive oil
1 tablespoon lemon juice
2 tablespoons orange juice
35 g (1/4 cup) currants
25 g (1/2 cup) finely chopped coriander
2 tablespoons finely chopped
   pistachio nuts
1 teaspoon orange flower water
250 g (1 cup) thick plain yoghurt

Peel and coarsely grate the carrots, and place in a large bowl.

Crush the cardamom pods to extract the seeds. Discard the pods. Heat a frying pan over low heat, and cook the mustard seeds for a few seconds, or until they start to pop. Add the cumin, ginger, paprika, cardamom and ground coriander, and heat for 5 seconds, or until fragrant. Remove from the heat and stir in the oil, juices and currants until combined.

Pour the dressing over the carrot and leave for 30 minutes. Add the fresh coriander and toss to combine. Pile the salad onto a serving dish and garnish with the chopped pistachios. Mix the orange flower water and yoghurt, and serve separately.

Serves 4–6

Mixed salad with warm Brie dressing

½ sourdough baguette
165 ml extra virgin olive oil
6 rashers streaky bacon
2 garlic cloves, peeled
2 baby cos lettuce
90 g (2 cups) baby English
  spinach leaves
80 g (½ cup) pine nuts, toasted
2 French shallots, finely chopped
1 tablespoon Dijon mustard
80 ml (⅓ cup) sherry vinegar
300 g ripe Brie cheese, rind removed

Preheat the oven to 180°C (350°F/ Gas 4). Thinly slice the baguette on the diagonal. Use 2 tablespoons of oil to brush both sides of each slice, place on a baking tray and bake for 20 minutes, or until golden.

Place the bacon on a separate tray and bake for 3–5 minutes, or until crisp. Remove the bread from the oven and use one clove of garlic to rub the bread slices. Break the bacon into pieces and leave to cool.

Remove the outer leaves of the cos lettuce. Rinse the inner leaves well, drain, dry and place in a large bowl with the spinach. Add the bacon, croutons and pine nuts.

Place the remaining olive oil in a frying pan and heat gently. Add the shallots and cook until they soften, then crush the remaining clove of garlic and add to the pan. Whisk in the mustard and vinegar, then gently whisk in the chopped Brie, until it has melted. Remove the dressing from the heat and, while it is still warm, pour over the salad and toss gently.

Serves 4

Vegetable skewers with salsa verde

Salsa verde
1 garlic clove
1 tablespoon capers, rinsed
and drained
20 g (1 cup) flat-leaf parsley
15 g (½ cup) basil leaves
10 g (½ cup) mint leaves
80 ml (⅓ cup) olive oil
1 teaspoon Dijon mustard
1 tablespoon red wine vinegar

16 small yellow squash (pattypan
squash)
16 baby carrots, peeled
16 French shallots, peeled
1 large red capsicum (pepper), halved
and cut into 2 cm thick slices
16 baby zucchini (courgettes)
2 garlic cloves, crushed
1 teaspoon chopped thyme
1 tablespoon olive oil
16 fresh bay or sage leaves

Soak 16 wooden skewers in cold water for 30 minutes to prevent them from burning during cooking.

To make the salsa verde, combine the garlic, capers and herbs in a food processor until the herbs are roughly chopped. With the motor running, pour the olive oil in a slow stream until incorporated. Combine the mustard with the red wine vinegar and stir through the salsa verde. Season. Cover with plastic wrap and refrigerate.

Blanch the vegetables separately in a large pot of boiling, salted water until just tender. Drain in a colander, then toss with the garlic, thyme and oil. Season well.

Thread the vegetables onto the skewers starting with a squash, then a French shallot, a bay leaf then the zucchini, carrot and capsicum. Repeat to make 16 skewers in total.

Place the skewers on a hot grill and cook for 3 minutes on each side, or until cooked and browned. Arrange on couscous or rice and serve with the salsa verde.

Serves 8

Roast tomato salad

6 Roma (plum) tomatoes
2 teaspoons capers, rinsed
  and drained
6 basil leaves, torn
1 tablespoon olive oil
1 tablespoon balsamic vinegar
2 garlic cloves, crushed
1/2 teaspoon honey

Cut the tomatoes lengthways into quarters. Place on a grill tray, skin-side-down, and cook under a hot grill for 4–5 minutes, or until golden. Cool to room temperature and place in a bowl.

Combine the capers, basil leaves, olive oil, balsamic vinegar, garlic cloves and honey in a bowl, season with salt and freshly ground black pepper, and pour over the tomatoes. Toss gently.

Serves 6

Bean salad

250 g green beans, trimmed
250 g yellow beans, trimmed
60 ml (¼ cup) olive oil
1 tablespoon lemon juice
1 garlic clove, crushed
shaved Parmesan cheese

Bring a saucepan of lightly salted water to the boil. Add the green and yellow beans, and cook for 2 minutes, or until just tender. Plunge into cold water and drain.

Place the olive oil, lemon juice and garlic in a bowl, season with salt and freshly ground black pepper, and mix together well. Place the beans in a serving bowl, pour on the dressing and toss to coat. Top with the Parmesan and serve.

Serves 6

Dill potato salad

600 g desiree potatoes
2 eggs
2 tablespoons finely chopped dill
1½ tablespoons finely chopped
    French shallots
1 egg yolk
2 teaspoons lemon juice
1 teaspoon Dijon mustard
100 ml light olive oil

Bring a large saucepan of water to the boil. Cook the potatoes for 20 minutes, or until tender. Add the eggs for the last 10 minutes. Remove the potatoes and eggs, and allow to cool. Peel the potatoes, then cut into 2–3 cm cubes. Peel and chop the eggs. Place in a large bowl with the dill, eggs and shallots. Toss to combine, then season.

Place the egg yolk, lemon juice, mustard and a pinch of salt in the bowl of a food processor. With the motor running, gradually add the olive oil a few drops at a time. When about half the oil has been added, pour in the remaining oil in a steady stream until it has all been incorporated. Use a large metal spoon to gently combine the potato and mayonnaise, then serve.

Serves 4

Beetroot and sweet potato salad with feta

350 g fresh baby beetroot, trimmed
    and washed
350 g orange sweet potato, peeled
    and cut into 2 cm chunks
60 ml (¼ cup) garlic oil (see Note)
1 garlic bulb
3 tablespoons olive oil
20 g butter
1 red onion, cut into 1 cm wedges
1 tablespoon balsamic vinegar
1 teaspoon soft brown sugar
2 tablespoons lemon juice
1 tablespoon shredded basil
150 g baby English spinach leaves
2 sprigs rosemary, leaves removed
    and stems discarded
120 g feta cheese

Preheat the oven to 180°C (350°F/ Gas 4). Wrap each beetroot in foil and place on a baking tray. Brush the sweet potato with garlic oil and season. Place on another baking tray with the whole garlic bulb. Cook with the beetroot for 35–40 minutes, or until tender. Test with a skewer, and when tender, remove from the oven and allow to cool.

Heat 1 tablespoon of olive oil and the butter in a small saucepan over medium heat until the butter has melted. Add the onion and cook, stirring occasionally, for 15 minutes, or until soft. Add the vinegar and sugar, and cook for 3–5 minutes, or until the onion is golden and starting to caramelise.

Peel the garlic cloves and combine them with the lemon juice, basil and remaining oil. Season to taste.

Toss the spinach, beetroot, sweet potato, onion and rosemary in a bowl. Crumble the feta over the top and drizzle with the dressing. Serve warm.

Serves 4

Note: If garlic oil is unavailable, you may make your own by steeping some crushed garlic in extra virgin olive oil for 2 hours, then straining, or use plain olive oil.

Caponata

1 kg eggplant (aubergine), cubed
185 ml (³/₄ cup) olive oil
200 g zucchini (courgettes), cubed
1 red capsicum (pepper), thinly sliced
2 onions, finely sliced
4 celery stalks, sliced
400 g tin crushed tomatoes
3 tablespoons red wine vinegar
2 tablespoons sugar
2 tablespoons capers, rinsed
  and drained
24 green olives, pitted
2 tablespoons pine nuts, toasted

Put the eggplant in a colander, add 2 teaspoons of salt and leave to drain.

Heat 3 tablespoons of the oil in a large frying pan and fry the zucchini and capsicum for 5–6 minutes, or until the zucchini is lightly browned. Transfer to a bowl. Add a little more oil to the pan and gently fry the onion and celery for 6–8 minutes, or until softened but not brown. Transfer to the bowl with the zucchini.

Rinse the eggplant and pat dry. Add 60 ml (¼ cup) of the oil to the pan, increase the heat and brown the eggplant in batches. Keep adding more oil to each batch. Drain on paper towels and set aside.

Remove any excess oil from the pan and return the vegetables to the pan, except the eggplant.

Add 60 ml (¼ cup) water and the tomatoes. Reduce the heat and simmer for 10 minutes. Add the remaining ingredients and eggplant and mix well. Remove from the heat and cool. Cover and leave for 24 hours in the refrigerator. Add some pepper, and more vinegar if needed.

Serves 8

Frisée and garlic crouton salad

Vinaigrette
1 French shallot, finely chopped
1 tablespoon Dijon mustard
60 ml (¼ cup) tarragon vinegar
170 ml (⅔ cup) extra virgin olive oil

1 tablespoon olive oil
250 g speck, rind removed, cut into
  5 mm x 2 cm pieces
½ baguette, sliced
4 garlic cloves
1 baby frisée (curly endive), washed
  and dried
100 g (½ cup) walnuts, toasted

For the vinaigrette, whisk together in a bowl the shallot, mustard and vinegar. Slowly add the oil, whisking constantly until thickened. Set aside.

Heat the oil in a large frying pan, add the speck, bread and garlic cloves and cook over medium–high heat for 5–8 minutes, until the bread and speck are both crisp. Remove the garlic from the pan.

Place the frisée, bread, speck, walnuts and vinaigrette in a large bowl. Toss together well and serve.

Serves 4–6

Sweets

Baked lemon cheesecake

100 g plain sweet biscuits, crushed
75 g butter, melted
300 g low-fat ricotta cheese
200 g light cream cheese
125 g (½ cup) caster sugar
80 ml (⅓ cup) lemon juice
2 tablespoons grated lemon zest
1 egg
1 egg white

Preheat the oven to 160°C (315°F/ Gas 2–3). Lightly grease an 18 cm springform tin and line the base with baking paper. Combine the crushed biscuits and butter and press into the base of the tin. Refrigerate for 30 minutes.

Beat the ricotta, cream cheese, sugar, lemon juice and 3 teaspoons of lemon zest with electric beaters until smooth. Beat in the egg and egg white.

Pour the mixture into the tin and sprinkle the surface with the remaining lemon zest. Bake for 45 minutes — the centre will still be a little wobbly. Leave to cool, then chill for 5 hours before serving.

Serves 8

Orchard fruit compote

90 g (¼ cup) honey
½ teaspoon ground ginger
1 cinnamon stick
3 whole cloves
pinch ground nutmeg
750 ml (3 cups) dessert wine
  such as Sauternes
1 lemon
6 pitted prunes
3 dried peaches, halved
5 dates, seeded and halved
10 dried apricots
1 lapsang souchong tea bag
2 golden delicious apples
2 beurre bosc pears
400 g Greek-style plain yoghurt

Place the honey, ginger, cinnamon stick, cloves, nutmeg and wine in a saucepan. Peel a large piece of zest from the lemon and place in the pan. Squeeze the juice from the lemon to give 60 ml (¼ cup) and add to the pan. Bring to the boil, stirring, then simmer for 20 minutes.

Meanwhile, place the prunes, peaches, dates and apricots in a large heatproof bowl. Cover with boiling water, add the tea bag and leave to soak. Peel and core the apples and pears, and cut into pieces about the same size as the dried fruits. Add to the syrup and allow to simmer for 8–10 minutes, or until tender. Drain the dried fruit and remove the tea bag, then add the fruit to the pan and cook for a further 5 minutes.

Remove all the fruit from the pan with a slotted spoon and place in a serving dish. Return the pan to the heat, bring to the boil, then reduce the heat and simmer for 6 minutes, or until the syrup has reduced by half. Pour over the fruit compote and chill for 30 minutes. Serve with the yoghurt.

Serves 4

Berries in Champagne jelly

1 litre Champagne or sparkling white
  wine
1 1/2 tablespoons gelatine
250 g (1 cup) sugar
4 strips lemon zest
4 strips orange zest
250 g (1 2/3 cups) small hulled and
  halved strawberries
255 g (1 2/3 cups) blueberries

Pour 500 ml (2 cups) Champagne into a bowl and let the bubbles subside. Sprinkle the gelatine over the Champagne in an even layer. Leave until the gelatine is spongy — do not stir. Place the remaining Champagne in a large saucepan with the sugar, lemon and orange zest, and heat gently, stirring constantly for 3–4 minutes, or until all of the sugar has dissolved.

Remove the pan from the heat, add the gelatine mixture and stir until thoroughly dissolved. Leave the jelly to cool completely, then remove the lemon and orange zest.

Divide the berries among eight 125 ml (1/2 cup) stemmed wine glasses and gently pour the jelly over the top. Refrigerate for 6 hours or overnight, or until the jelly has fully set. Remove from the refrigerator 15 minutes before serving.

Serves 8

Macaroon berry trifle

420 ml (1²/₃ cups) skim milk
2 tablespoons caster sugar
1 teaspoon natural vanilla essence
2¹/₂ tablespoons custard powder
1 tablespoon Marsala
2 teaspoons instant coffee powder
16 amaretti biscuits, roughly broken
2 tablespoons orange juice
200 g fresh raspberries
425 g tin pears in natural juice,
    drained, roughly chopped

vanilla ice cream

Place the milk, sugar and vanilla in a heavy-based saucepan and cook over low heat, stirring occasionally. Combine the custard powder with 2 tablespoons of water, mix to a smooth paste and whisk into the milk mixture until the custard boils and thickens. Remove from the heat and cover with plastic wrap, placing it directly on the surface of the custard to prevent any skin forming, and allow to cool.

Place the Marsala and coffee powder in a small bowl and stir until the coffee has dissolved. Place the biscuits and orange juice in a large bowl and stir to coat the biscuits. Layer half of the biscuit in the base of four serving glasses and drizzle with the Marsala mixture. Top with a third of the berries and half of the pear, then pour in half of the custard. Repeat the layering, finishing with the raspberries. Refrigerate the trifles for 10 minutes or serve immediately with a scoop of vanilla ice cream.

Serves 4

Chocolate and raspberry ice cream sandwich

300 g frozen chocolate pound cake
2 tablespoons raspberry liqueur,
  optional
250 g (2 cups) fresh or thawed
  raspberries
250 g (1 cup) sugar
1 teaspoon lemon juice
1 litre vanilla ice cream, softened
icing sugar, to dust

Using a sharp knife, cut the pound cake lengthwise into four thin slices. Using a 6.5 cm plain cutter, cut eight rounds from the slices of cake. You will need two rounds of cake per person. Brush each round with half of the raspberry liqueur if using, then cover and set aside.

Line a 20 x 20 cm tin or dish with baking paper, leaving a generous overhang of paper on two opposite sides. Place the raspberries, sugar, lemon juice and remaining liqueur in a blender and blend to a smooth purée. Reserving 125 ml ($1/2$ cup) of the purée, fold the remainder through the ice cream and pour into the tin. Freeze for 2 hours, or until firm.

Remove the ice cream from the freezer and use the overhanging baking paper to lift from the tin. Using a 6.5 cm cutter, cut four rounds from the ice cream.

To assemble, place four slices of cake on a tray, top each with a round of ice cream and then the remaining slices of cake. Smooth the sides of the ice cream to neaten, if necessary. Return the sandwiches to the freezer for 5 minutes to firm. Dust with icing sugar and serve with the remaining raspberry sauce.

Serves 4

Mango sorbet

375 g (1 ½ cups) caster sugar
125 ml (½ cup) lime juice
5 fresh mangoes (1.5 kg)

Place the sugar in a saucepan with 625 ml (2 ½ cups) water. Stir over low heat until the sugar dissolves, then bring to the boil. Reduce to a simmer for 15 minutes, then stir in the juice.

Peel the mangoes and remove the flesh from the stone. Chop and place in a heatproof bowl. Add the syrup and leave to cool.

Place the mango mixture in a blender, blend until smooth, then pour into a shallow metal dish and freeze for 1 hour, or until it starts to freeze around the edges. Return to the blender and blend until smooth. Pour back into the tray and return to the freezer. Repeat three times. For the final freezing, place in an airtight container and cover the sorbet with a piece of greaseproof paper and lid. Allow the sorbet to soften slightly before serving with tropical fruit.

Serves 4

Note: You can use frozen mango if fresh is unavailable. Use 1 kg frozen mango cheeks, softened, 185 g (¾ cup) caster sugar and 60 ml (¼ cup) lime juice, and follow the method as above.

Lemon grass and ginger infused fruit salad

60 g (¼ cup) caster sugar
2 cm x 2 cm piece fresh ginger, thinly
  sliced
1 stalk lemon grass, bruised and
  halved
1 large passionfruit
1 red pawpaw
½ honeydew melon
1 large mango
1 small fresh pineapple
12 fresh lychees
5 g (¼ cup) mint leaves, shredded

Place the sugar, ginger and lemon grass in a small saucepan, add 125 ml (½ cup) water and stir over low heat to dissolve the sugar. Boil for 5 minutes, or until reduced to 80 ml (⅓ cup) and cool. Strain the syrup and add the passionfruit pulp.

Peel and seed the pawpaw and melon. Cut into 4 cm cubes. Peel the mango and cut the flesh into cubes, discarding the stone. Peel, halve and core the pineapple and cut into cubes. Peel the lychees, then make a slit in the flesh and remove the seed.

Place all the fruit in a large serving bowl. Pour on the syrup, or serve separately if preferred. Garnish with the shredded mint.

Serves 4

Choc-chip banana ice

600 ml ready-made low-fat custard
2 ripe bananas, mashed
2 teaspoons lemon juice
50 g dark chocolate

Combine the custard, mashed banana and lemon juice in a large mixing bowl. Beat with electric beaters until the banana and custard are well combined, with no lumps of banana remaining.

Pour into a metal cake tin, cover with plastic wrap and freeze for 3–4 hours, or until semi-frozen. Transfer to a chilled bowl and beat for 2 minutes with electric beaters until slushy, then return to the cake tin and place in the freezer for 2–3 hours, or until almost firm. Repeat the freezing and beating twice more (for a total of three times).

Finely chop the chocolate and fold into the mixture after the last beating. Refreeze in an airtight plastic container. Remove from the freezer and allow the ice cream to soften slightly before serving.

Serves 6

Cassata

30 g crystallised ginger, finely
chopped
50 g red glacé cherries, roughly
chopped or sliced
300 g low-fat vanilla ice cream,
softened
250 g frozen strawberry fruit dessert,
softened
300 g low-fat chocolate ice cream,
softened

Line a 1.25 litre rectangular tin with plastic wrap, leaving an overhang on the sides.

Stir the ginger and glacé cherries into the vanilla ice cream until well combined. Spoon into the prepared tin and smooth down. Freeze for 1 hour, or until firm.

Spoon the strawberry fruit dessert over the ice cream mixture, smooth the surface and return to the freezer for another hour.

Spoon the chocolate ice cream over the strawberry, smoothing the surface. Cover with plastic wrap, and freeze for at least 3 hours or overnight. To serve, plunge the bottom of the tin into warm water for 10 seconds to loosen and lift out using the plastic wrap. Cut into slices and serve.

Serves 10–12

Summer pudding

150 g blackcurrants
150 g redcurrants
150 g raspberries
150 g blackberries
200 g strawberries, hulled and
  quartered or halved
125 g (½ cup) caster sugar, or
  to taste
6–8 slices good-quality sliced white
  bread, crusts removed

Put all the berries except the strawberries in a saucepan with 125 ml (½ cup) water and heat for 5 minutes, or until the berries begin to soften. Add the strawberries and remove from the heat. Add sugar, to taste (how much you need will depend on how ripe the fruit is). Cool.

Line six 170 ml (⅔ cup) moulds or a 1 litre pudding basin with the bread. For the small moulds cut a circle to fit the bottom and strips to fit around the sides. For the basin, cut a large circle out of one slice for the bottom and cut the rest of the bread into strips to fit the side. Drain a little of the juice off the fruit. Dip one side of each piece of bread in the juice before fitting it, juice-side-down, into the basin, leaving no gaps. Do not squeeze the bread or it will not absorb the juice.

Fill each mould with fruit and add some juice. Cover the top with the remaining dipped bread, juice-side up. Cover with plastic wrap. For the small moulds, sit a small tin on top of each. For the basin, sit a small plate onto the plastic wrap, then weigh it down with a large tin. Place on a tray to catch any juice which may overflow, and chill overnight. Carefully turn out the pudding and serve with leftover fruit mixture and cream if desired.

Serves 6

White chocolate mousse

100 g white chocolate melts (buttons)
125 ml (½ cup) skim milk
2 teaspoons gelatine
400 g low-fat French vanilla fromage
  frais or whipped yoghurt
3 egg whites
3 tablespoons passionfruit pulp
icing sugar, to dust

Place the chocolate and milk in a small saucepan and stir over low heat until the chocolate has melted. Allow to cool. Place 60 ml (¼ cup) boiling water in a heatproof bowl, sprinkle evenly with the gelatine, and stir until dissolved. Using a wooden spoon, stir the gelatine into the chocolate mixture.

Place the fromage frais in a large bowl and gradually stir in the chocolate mixture, a little at a time, stirring until smooth after each addition.

Beat the egg whites in a clean, dry bowl with electric beaters until soft peaks form. Gently fold the egg whites and the passionfruit pulp into the chocolate mixture. Divide the mixture equally among eight 125 ml (½ cup) serving dishes or a 1 litre glass bowl. Refrigerate for 3 hours, or until set. Serve with a light dusting of icing sugar.

Serves 8

Note: It is important to have the ingredients at room temperature to ensure the texture is smooth.

Watermelon granita

250 g (1 cup) caster sugar
1.5 kg watermelon

Place the sugar in a saucepan with 250 ml (1 cup) water and stir over low heat without boiling until the sugar has completely dissolved. Increase the heat and bring to the boil, then reduce the heat and simmer, without stirring, for 5 minutes. Pour into a large bowl to cool.

Remove the rind from the watermelon and place chunks of flesh in a food processor. Process until puréed, then strain to remove the seeds and fibre. Mix the watermelon purée with the sugar syrup, and pour into a shallow metal dish. Freeze for 1 hour, or until just frozen around the edges. Scrape this back into the mixture with a fork.

Repeat scraping the frozen edges every hour, at least twice more, or until the mixture has even-sized ice crystals. Serve immediately or beat well with a fork and refreeze just before serving. To serve, scrape the granita into serving dishes with a fork, or serve in scoops in a tall glass.

Serves 4

Variation: For refreshing extra flavour, add 2 tablespoons chopped mint when freezing the last time.

Almond semifreddo

300 ml cream
4 eggs, at room temperature,
　separated
85 g (^{2}/$_3$ cup) icing sugar
60 ml (^{1}/$_4$ cup) Amaretto
80 g (^{1}/$_2$ cup) blanched almonds,
　toasted and chopped
8 amaretti biscuits, crushed

fresh fruit or extra Amaretto

Whip the cream until firm peaks form, cover and chill. Line a 10 x 21 cm loaf tin with plastic wrap so that it overhangs the two long sides.

Place the egg yolks and icing sugar in a large bowl and beat until pale and creamy. Whisk the egg whites in a separate bowl until firm peaks form. Stir the Amaretto, almonds and amaretti biscuits into the egg yolk mixture, then carefully fold in the chilled cream and the egg whites until well combined. Carefully pour or spoon into the lined loaf tin and cover with the overhanging plastic. Freeze for 4 hours, or until frozen but not rock hard. Serve in slices with fresh fruit or a sprinkling of Amaretto. The semifreddo can also be poured into individual moulds or serving dishes before freezing.

Serves 8–10

Note: Semifreddo means semi-frozen, so if you want to leave it in the freezer overnight, remove it and place it in the refrigerator for 30 minutes to soften slightly before serving.

Petite custard tarts

3 sheets ready-made shortcrust
  pastry
250 ml (1 cup) skim milk
1 tablespoon custard powder
60 g (¼ cup) caster sugar
1 teaspoon vanilla essence
80 ml (⅓ cup) passionfruit pulp
½ teaspoon gelatine powder

Preheat the oven to 180°C (350°F/
Gas 4). Cut 12 circles from the pastry
sheets using an 8 cm round cutter.
Gently press into 12 patty tins (6 cm
diameter x 2.5 cm deep) and prick
each round with a fork.

Cut out a 5 cm square of foil for each
case and press into the pastry cases.
Bake for 10 minutes, remove the foil
and bake for 5 minutes, or until golden
and cooked through. Cool on a rack.

Mix 1 tablespoon of the milk and the
custard powder until smooth. Stir the
sugar, vanilla and remaining milk over
medium heat for 1 minute, or until
the sugar dissolves. Stir in the
custard mixture and cook, stirring,
for 2–3 minutes, or until thick. Cover
the surface of the custard with plastic
wrap. Cool to room temperature.

Place the passionfruit in a heatproof
bowl and sprinkle with gelatine. Leave
until the gelatine is spongy. Bring a
saucepan of water to the boil, remove
from the heat and place the bowl
in the pan. Stir until the gelatine
dissolves, then leave to cool. Divide
the custard among the pastry cases.
Top each with 1 teaspoon of the
passionfruit glaze and chill for at
least 2 hours.

Makes 12

Individual zucotto

450 g packet Madeira cake
60 ml (¼ cup) Cointreau
60 ml (¼ cup) brandy
300 ml thick (double) cream
3 teaspoons icing sugar, sifted
80 g (½ cup) blanched almonds,
    roasted, roughly chopped
70 g (½ cup) hazelnuts, roasted,
    roughly chopped
150 g good-quality dark chocolate,
    finely chopped

Cut the cake into 5 mm slices. Lightly grease six 150 ml ramekins and line with plastic wrap, leaving enough to hang over the sides. Press the pieces of the cake into the ramekins, overlapping to cover the base and sides. Combine the Cointreau and brandy in a bowl. Brush the cake with half the Cointreau mixture.

Place the cream and icing sugar in a bowl, and, using electric beaters, beat until firm and stiff. Fold in the nuts, chocolate and 1½ teaspoons Cointreau mixture. The mixture will be quite stiff.

Spoon the mixture into each ramekin and smooth over the surface. Cover with the overhanging plastic wrap and refrigerate for 2 hours or overnight. To serve, use the plastic wrap to lift the zucotto out of the ramekins, turn upside-down onto serving plates and brush with the remaining Cointreau mixture.

Serves 6

Apple and pear sorbet

4 large green apples, peeled, cored
  and chopped
4 pears, peeled, cored and chopped
1 piece of lemon zest (1.5 cm x 4 cm)
1 cinnamon stick
60 ml (¼ cup) lemon juice
4 tablespoons caster sugar
2 tablespoons Calvados or poire
  William liqueur, optional

Place the apple and pear in a large deep saucepan with the lemon zest, cinnamon stick and enough water to just cover the fruit. Cover and poach the fruit gently over medium–low heat for 6–8 minutes, or until tender. Remove the lemon zest and cinnamon stick. Place the fruit in a food processor and blend with the lemon juice until smooth.

Place the sugar in a saucepan with 80 ml (⅓ cup) water, bring to the boil and simmer for 1 minute. Add the fruit purée and the liqueur and combine.

Pour into a shallow metal tray and freeze for 2 hours, or until the mixture is frozen around the edges. Transfer to a food processor or bowl and blend or beat until just smooth. Pour back into the tray and return to the freezer. Repeat this process three times. For the final freezing, place in an airtight container, cover the surface with a piece of greaseproof paper and cover with a lid. Serve in small glasses or bowls.

Serves 4–6

Notes: Pour an extra nip of Calvados over the sorbet to serve, if desired.

Spiced poached pears

6 beurre bosc pears
300 ml rosé wine
150 ml good-quality apple or pear
  juice
4 cloves
1 vanilla bean, halved
1 cinnamon stick
1 tablespoon maple syrup
200 g low-fat vanilla yoghurt

Peel, halve and core the pears. Place in a deep frying pan with a lid, and add the wine, fruit juice and cloves. Scrape the seeds out of the vanilla bean and add both the seeds and pod to the pan. Stir in the cinnamon stick and maple syrup. Bring to the boil, then reduce the heat and simmer for 5–7 minutes, or until the pears are tender. Remove from the heat and cover with the lid.

Leave the fruit for 30 minutes to allow the flavours to infuse, then remove the pears with a slotted spoon and place in a serving dish. Return the syrup to the heat and boil for 6–8 minutes, or until reduced by half. Strain the syrup over the pears. Serve warm or chilled with the yoghurt.

Serves 6

Ginger and lychee jelly

565 g tin lychees
500 ml (2 cups) clear apple juice
  (no added sugar)
80 ml (⅓ cup) strained lime juice
2 tablespoons caster sugar
3 cm x 3 cm piece fresh ginger,
  peeled and thinly sliced
4 sheets gelatine (about 5 g)

mint leaves

Drain the syrup from the lychees and reserve 250 ml (1 cup) of the syrup. Discard the remaining syrup. Place the reserved syrup, apple juice, lime juice, sugar and ginger in a saucepan. Bring to the boil, then reduce the heat and simmer for 5 minutes. Strain into a heatproof bowl.

Place the gelatine sheets in a bowl of cold water and soak for 2 minutes, or until they soften. Squeeze out the excess water, then add to the syrup. Stir until the gelatine has completely dissolved. Leave to cool.

Pour 2 tablespoons of the jelly mixture into each of six 150 ml stemmed wine glasses, and divide the lychees among the wine glasses. Refrigerate until the jelly has set. Spoon the remaining jelly over the fruit and refrigerate until set. Before serving, garnish with mint leaves.

Serves 6

Peaches poached in wine

4 just-ripe yellow-fleshed freestone
  peaches
500 ml (2 cups) dessert wine such
  as Sauternes
60 ml (¼ cup) orange liqueur
250 g (1 cup) sugar
1 cinnamon stick
1 vanilla bean, split
8 mint leaves

mascarpone cheese or crème fraîche

Cut a small cross in the base of each peach. Immerse the peaches in boiling water for 30 seconds, then drain and cool slightly. Peel off the skin, cut in half and carefully remove the stones.

Place the wine, liqueur, sugar, cinnamon stick and vanilla bean in a deep-sided frying pan large enough to hold the peach halves in a single layer. Heat the mixture, stirring, until the sugar dissolves. Bring to the boil, then reduce the heat and simmer for 5 minutes. Add the peaches to the pan and simmer for 4 minutes, turning them over halfway through. Remove with a slotted spoon and leave to cool. Continue to simmer the syrup for 6–8 minutes, or until thick. Strain and set aside.

Arrange the peaches on a serving platter, cut-side-up. Spoon the syrup over the top and garnish each half with a mint leaf. Serve the peaches warm or chilled, with a dollop of mascarpone or crème fraîche.

Serves 4

Lemon granita

315 ml (1¼ cups) lemon juice
1 tablespoon lemon zest
200 g caster sugar

Place the lemon juice, lemon zest and caster sugar in a small saucepan and stir over low heat for 5 minutes, or until the sugar is dissolved. Remove from the heat and leave to cool.

Add 500 ml (2 cups) water to the juice mixture and mix together well. Pour the mixture into a shallow 30 x 20 cm metal container and place in the freezer until the mixture is beginning to freeze around the edges. Scrape the frozen sections back into the mixture with a fork. Repeat every 30 minutes until the mixture has even-size ice crystals. Beat the mixture with a fork just before serving. To serve, spoon the lemon granita into six chilled glasses.

Serves 6

Pannacotta with blueberry compote

300 ml low-fat milk
1 vanilla bean, halved
1 cinnamon stick
1/2 teaspoon vanilla essence
1 tablespoon caster sugar
2 sheets gelatine
200 g plain yoghurt

Blueberry compote
150 g fresh blueberries
15 g caster sugar
100 ml good-quality Marsala
1 cinnamon stick
2 cm strip lemon peel, white pith removed
1/2 vanilla bean, halved
1/2 teaspoon arrowroot

Pour the milk into a heavy-based saucepan. Scrape in the seeds from the vanilla bean and add the pod, cinnamon stick, vanilla essence and the sugar. Bring to the boil, stirring, then remove from the heat and leave to infuse for 10 minutes.

Soak the gelatine in cold water for 5 minutes, or until soft. Squeeze out and add the leaves to the milk. Stir over low heat until the leaves dissolve (do not boil). Remove the vanilla pod and the cinnamon stick. Cool to room temperature. Whisk in the yoghurt. Pour into four 125 ml (1/2 cup) ramekins and chill for 6 hours, or until set.

Place the berries in a saucepan and add the sugar, Marsala, cinnamon stick and peel. Scrape in the seeds from the vanilla bean and add the pod. Cook over low heat for 15 minutes, stirring occasionally. Make sure the fruit does not break up. Mix the arrowroot with 2 teaspoons water and add to the fruit. Cook, stirring, until the mixture thickens. Leave to cool for at least 2 hours.

Run a knife around the edge of each ramekin and invert the pannacotta onto plates. Remove the cinnamon, peel and pod from the compote, and serve with the pannacotta.

Serves 4

Chocolate mousse

100 g dark chocolate
60 ml (¼ cup) evaporated skim milk
2 tablespoons cocoa powder
¼ teaspoon rosewater essence or
   2 teaspoons vanilla essence
125 g (½ cup) caster sugar
3 egg whites
cocoa powder, to dust

savoiardi (sponge finger biscuits)

Chop the chocolate into small, even pieces and place in a heatproof bowl with the milk and cocoa powder. Bring a saucepan of water to the boil, then reduce the heat to a gentle simmer. Sit the bowl over the saucepan, making sure the base of the bowl does not touch the water. Stir once, if necessary, to ensure even melting. When completely melted, mix until smooth, then stir in the rosewater essence and leave to cool.

Place the sugar and 80 ml (⅓ cup) water in a small, heavy-based saucepan, and stir over low heat until the sugar has dissolved. Bring to a simmer, without stirring, for 5 minutes, or until a small amount of the syrup placed in a saucer of water forms a soft ball. Remove from the heat.

Meanwhile, using electric beaters, beat the egg whites in a clean, dry bowl until soft peaks form. With the beater on medium, gradually add the hot sugar syrup, then beat on high speed for 3–4 minutes, or until the meringue is very thick and glossy. Gently fold in the cooled chocolate mixture, then pour into four 160 ml serving glasses. Chill for at least 4 hours. Dust with cocoa and serve with a sponge finger biscuit.

Serves 4

Drinks

Earl Grey summer tea

1 cinnamon stick
1 tablespoon Earl Grey tea leaves
250 ml (1 cup) orange juice
2 teaspoons finely grated orange zest
2 tablespoons sugar, to taste
ice cubes
1 orange, sliced into thin rounds

4 cinnamon sticks

Place the cinnamon stick, tea leaves, orange juice, orange zest and 750 ml (3 cups) water in a medium pan.

Slowly bring to a simmer over gentle heat. Once simmering, stir in the sugar, to taste, and stir until dissolved. Remove from the heat and allow to cool. Once the mixture has cooled, strain the liquid into a jug and refrigerate until cold.

Serve in a jug with lots of ice cubes, and garnish with the orange slices and extra cinnamon stick.

Makes 4 x 250 ml glasses

Lemon, lime and soda with citrus ice cubes

1 lemon
1 lime
2½ tablespoons lemon juice
170 ml (⅔ cup) lime juice cordial
625 ml (2½ cups) soda water, chilled

Using a sharp knife, remove the peel and white pith from the lemon and lime. On a chopping board, cut between the membranes to release the segments. Place a lemon and lime segment in each hole of an ice cube tray and cover with water. Freeze for 2–3 hours or overnight until firm.

Combine the lemon juice, lime juice cordial and soda water.

Pour into long, chilled glasses with the ice cubes.

Makes 2 x 375 ml glasses and 8 ice cubes

Passionfruit and vanilla ice cream whip

4 passionfruit
100 g passionfruit yoghurt
500 ml (2 cups) milk
1 tablespoon caster sugar
2 scoops vanilla ice cream

Scoop out the pulp from the passionfruit and push through a sieve to remove the seeds. Place into the blender with the yoghurt, milk, sugar and ice cream and blend until smooth.

Pour into tall glasses and serve with an extra scoop of ice cream, if desired.

Makes 2 x 375 ml glasses

Melon shake

500 g rockmelon, peeled and seeded
2 tablespoons honey
375 ml (1 1/2 cups) milk
5 scoops vanilla ice cream

ground nutmeg

Cut the rockmelon into 2 cm pieces and place in a blender. Mix for 30 seconds, or until smooth.

Add the honey, milk and ice cream and blend the mixture for a further 10–20 seconds, or until well combined and smooth. Serve sprinkled with nutmeg.

Makes 2 x 375 ml glasses

Coconut and lime lassi

400 ml coconut milk
185 g (³/₄ cup) plain yoghurt
60 ml (¹/₄ cup) lime juice
60 g (¹/₄ cup) caster sugar
8–10 ice cubes

lime slices

Blend together the coconut milk, yoghurt, lime juice, sugar and ice cubes until the mixture is well combined and the ice cubes are well crushed.

Pour into tall glasses and serve immediately, garnished with slices of fresh lime.

Makes 2 x 375 ml glasses

Peachy egg nog

2 eggs, separated
60 ml (¼ cup) milk
60 g (¼ cup) caster sugar
80 ml (⅓ cup) cream
440 ml (1¾ cups) peach nectar
2 tablespoons orange juice

ground nutmeg

Beat the egg yolks, milk and half the sugar in a bowl and place over a pan of simmering water — do not allow the base of the bowl to touch the water. Cook, stirring, for 8 minutes, or until the custard thickens. Remove from the heat and cover the surface with plastic wrap. Cool.

Beat the egg whites until frothy. Add the remaining sugar, to taste, then beat until stiff peaks form. In a separate bowl, whip the cream until soft peaks form.

Gently fold the egg whites and cream into the cooled custard. Stir in the nectar and juice. Cover and chill for 2 hours.

Beat the mixture lightly, pour into glasses and sprinkle with nutmeg.

Makes 4 x 225 ml glasses

Cranberry and vanilla ice cream spider

500 ml (2 cups) cranberry juice
500 ml (2 cups) soda water
4 scoops vanilla ice cream
185 ml (3/4 cup) cream
1 tablespoon caster sugar
20 g flaked almonds, toasted

Combine the juice and soda water in a jug. Add a scoop of ice cream to each tall glass. Pour the juice and soda over the ice cream.

Whip the cream and sugar until soft peaks form. Spoon over the juice and soda and top with a sprinkle of almonds.

Makes 4 x 250 ml glasses

Summer buttermilk smoothie

350 g rockmelon
2 peaches, peeled and sliced
150 g strawberries, roughly chopped
4 mint leaves
125 ml (½ cup) buttermilk
125 ml (½ cup) orange juice
1–2 tablespoons honey

Remove the zest and seeds from the melon and cut the flesh into pieces.

Place the rockmelon, peaches, strawberries and mint leaves in a blender and blend until smooth.

Add the buttermilk, orange juice and 1 tablespoon of the honey and blend to combine. Taste for sweetness and add more honey if needed.

Makes 2 x 375 ml glasses

Note: This drink should be consumed within 3 hours of being made or it will lose colour and freshness of flavour.

Blackcurrant crush

750 ml (3 cups) apple and
  blackcurrant juice
500 ml (2 cups) soda water
1 tablespoon caster sugar
150 g blueberries
ice cubes

Place the apple and blackcurrant juice, soda water, sugar and blueberries into a blender and blend until smooth.

Serve in chilled glasses over ice.

Makes 4 x 300 ml glasses

Note: If you have a really good blender, you may wish to add the ice cubes when blending the other ingredients to make a slushy.

Apricot whip

75 g dried apricots
125 g (½ cup) apricot yoghurt
170 ml (⅔ cup) light coconut milk
315 ml (1¼ cups) milk
1 tablespoon honey
1 scoop vanilla ice cream

flaked coconut, toasted

Cover the apricots with boiling water and soak for 15 minutes. Drain and roughly chop. Place the apricots, yoghurt, coconut milk, milk, honey and ice cream in a blender and blend until smooth.

Pour into tall, chilled glasses and sprinkle with the flaked coconut.

Makes 3 x 250 ml glasses

Chocoholic thickshake

125 ml (½ cup) cold milk
50 g dark chocolate, grated
2 tablespoons chocolate syrup
2 tablespoons cream
4 scoops chocolate ice cream
2 scoops chocolate ice cream, extra

grated dark chocolate

Blend the milk, chocolate, syrup, cream and ice cream in a blender until smooth.

Pour into chilled glasses. Top each glass with a scoop of ice cream and sprinkle with grated chocolate.

Makes 2 x 250 ml glasses

Banana date smoothie

250 g (1 cup) low-fat plain yoghurt
125 ml (½ cup) skim milk
50 g (½ cup) fresh dates, stoned
  and chopped
2 bananas, sliced
8 ice cubes

Place the yoghurt, milk, dates,
banana and ice cubes in a blender.
Blend until the mixture is smooth
and the ice cubes have been well
incorporated.

Serve in chilled glasses.

Makes 2 x 350 ml glasses

Orange and cardamom herbal tea

3 cardamom pods
250 ml (1 cup) orange juice
3 strips orange zest
2 tablespoons caster sugar

Place the cardamom pods on a chopping board and press with the side of a large knife to crack them open. Place the cardamom, orange juice, zest, sugar and 500 ml (2 cups) water in a pan and stir over medium heat for 10 minutes, or until the sugar has dissolved. Bring to the boil then remove from the heat.

Leave to infuse for 2–3 hours, or until cold. Chill in the refrigerator. Strain and serve over ice.

Makes 2 x 275 ml glasses

Virgin Mary

750 ml (3 cups) tomato juice
2 tablespoons lemon juice
1 tablespoon Worcestershire sauce
1/4 teaspoon ground nutmeg
few drops Tabasco sauce
1 cup ice (12 ice cubes)
2 lemon slices, halved

Place the tomato juice, lemon juice,
Worcestershire sauce, nutmeg and
Tabasco sauce in a large jug and
stir until combined.

Place the ice cubes in a blender and
blend for 30 seconds, or until the ice
is crushed down to 1/2 cup.

Pour the tomato juice mixture into
serving glasses and add the crushed
ice and lemon slices. Season with salt
and pepper before serving.

Makes 4 x 200 ml glasses

Mandarin and mango chill

1 mango, cut into slices
500 ml (2 cups) mandarin juice
125 ml (½ cup) lime juice cordial
375 ml (1½ cups) soda water
2 tablespoons caster sugar
ice cubes

Freeze the mango for about 1 hour, or until semi-frozen.

Combine the juice, cordial, soda water and sugar in a jug.

Place the mango slices and some ice cubes into each glass, then pour in the juice mix.

Makes 2 x 375 ml glasses

Very berry

250 g (1 cup) low-fat strawberry
  yoghurt
125 ml (½ cup) cranberry juice, chilled
250 g strawberries, hulled and
  quartered
125 g frozen raspberries

Combine the yoghurt and cranberry juice in a blender. Add the quartered strawberries and 80 g of the raspberries. Blend until smooth.

Pour into chilled glasses and top with the remaining frozen raspberries. Serve with a spoon as it is quite thick.

Makes 4 x 200 ml glasses

Summer strawberry smoothie

1 tablespoon strawberry flavouring
250 ml (1 cup) wildberry drinking
  yoghurt
250 g strawberries, hulled
4 scoops frozen strawberry yoghurt
few drops vanilla essence
ice cubes

Combine the strawberry flavouring, drinking yoghurt, strawberries, frozen yoghurt and vanilla in a blender and process until smooth.

Pour over lots of ice to serve.

Makes 2 x 300 ml glasses

Big bold banana

750 ml (3 cups) soy milk, chilled
125 g soft silken tofu
4 very ripe bananas, sliced
1 tablespoon honey
1 tablespoon vanilla essence
1 tablespoon cocoa powder

Combine the soy milk and tofu in a blender. Add the banana, honey, vanilla essence and cocoa powder. Blend until smooth.

Serve in tall chilled glasses with a long spoon.

Makes 4 x 375 ml glasses

Orange and ginger tea cooler

1 small orange
½–1 tablespoon Darjeeling tea leaves
250 ml (1 cup) ginger beer
8 thin slices glacé ginger
2 tablespoons sugar
4–6 ice cubes

mint leaves

Remove the peel from the orange using a vegetable peeler, avoiding the white pith, and cut into long thin strips. Place half the peel and the tea leaves in a bowl and pour in 500 ml (2 cups) boiling water. Cover and leave to steep for 5 minutes, then strain through a fine strainer.

Pour into a jug, add the ginger beer and chill for 6 hours, or overnight if possible.

One hour before serving, add the ginger, sugar and remaining orange peel. Stir well.

Pour into tall glasses, add 2–3 ice cubes per glass and garnish with mint leaves.

Makes 2 x 375 ml glasses

Lemon barley water

110 g (½ cup) pearl barley
3 lemons
125 g (½ cup) caster sugar
crushed ice

lemon slices

Wash the barley well and place in a medium pan. Using a sharp vegetable peeler, remove the peel from the lemons, avoiding the bitter white pith. Squeeze out the juice and set aside. Add the peel and 1.75 litres cold water to the barley and bring to the boil. Simmer briskly for 30 minutes. Add the sugar and mix to dissolve. Allow to cool.

Strain the liquid into a jug and add the lemon juice. Serve over crushed ice and garnish with lemon slices.

Makes 4 x 250 ml glasses

Homemade lemonade

685 ml (2¾ cups) lemon juice
310 g (1¼ cups) sugar
ice cubes

mint leaves

Combine the lemon juice and sugar in a large bowl, stirring until the sugar has dissolved. Pour into a large jug.

Add 1.25 litres water to the jug, stirring well to combine. Chill.

To serve, pour over ice cubes and garnish with mint leaves.

Makes 6 x 375 ml glasses

Banana passion

3 passionfruit, halved
1 large banana, chopped
250 ml (1 cup) skim milk
60 g (¼ cup) low-fat plain yoghurt

Scoop out the passionfruit pulp and place in a blender. Add the banana, milk and yoghurt and blend, turning quickly on and off (or use the pulse button), until smooth and the seeds are finely chopped. (Add more milk if it is too thick.) Don't blend for too long or it will become very bubbly and increase in volume.

Makes 2 x 250 ml glasses

Smoothberry

150 g strawberries, hulled
60 g raspberries
200 g boysenberries
250 ml (1 cup) milk
3 scoops vanilla ice cream

Place the strawberries, raspberries, boysenberries, milk and ice cream in a blender and blend until smooth, then chill.

Pour into chilled glasses and serve.

Makes 4 x 200 ml glasses

Note: If boysenberries are unavailable, any other berry can be used.

Iced chocolate

2 tablespoons rich chocolate topping
375 ml (1½ cups) icy-cold milk
1 scoop vanilla ice cream

whipped cream
drinking chocolate

Pour the chocolate topping into a glass and swirl it around the sides. Fill with the cold milk and add the ice cream.

Serve with a big swirl of whipped cream and dust with drinking chocolate.

Makes 1 x 375 ml glass

Lemon grass tea

3 stalks lemon grass
2 slices lemon
3 teaspoons honey, or to taste

lemon slices

Prepare the lemon grass by removing the first two tough outer layers. For maximum flavour, only use the bottom one-third of the stalk (the white part). Slice thinly into rings. (You could use the remaining stalks as a garnish, if you like.)

Place the lemon grass in a jug and cover with 2½ cups (625 ml) boiling water. Add the lemon slices and cover. Allow to infuse and cool. When cooled to room temperature, strain. Add the honey, to taste. Place the tea in the refrigerator to chill.

To serve, pour the tea into two glasses with extra slices of lemon. Add ice, if desired.

Makes 2 x 310 ml glasses

Raspberry lemonade

300 g fresh or frozen raspberries,
  thawed
310 g (1 1/4 cups) sugar
500 ml (2 cups) lemon juice
ice cubes

mint leaves

Combine the raspberries and sugar in a blender and blend until smooth.

Place a strong sieve over a large bowl and push the mixture through to remove the seeds. Discard the seeds.

Add the lemon juice and mix well. Pour into a large jug and stir in 1.5 litres water, then chill.

To serve, pour over ice cubes and garnish with mint leaves.

Makes 6 x 375 ml glasses

Coconut and passionfruit smoothie

140 ml coconut milk
250 ml (1 cup) milk
25 g (¼ cup) desiccated coconut
¼ teaspoon natural vanilla essence
3 scoops vanilla ice cream
170 g tin passionfruit pulp in syrup

Blend together the coconut milk, milk, coconut, vanilla, ice cream and half the passionfruit pulp until the mixture is smooth and fluffy.

Stir in the remaining pulp and serve immediately.

Makes 2 x 375 ml glasses

Sports shake

500 ml (2 cups) milk, chilled
2 tablespoons honey
2 eggs
½ teaspoon vanilla essence
1 tablespoon wheat germ
1 medium banana, sliced

Blend the milk, honey, eggs, vanilla, wheat germ and banana until smooth.

Chill well and serve.

Makes 2 x 250 ml glasses

Iced mint tea

4 peppermint tea bags
115 g (⅓ cup) honey
500 ml (2 cups) grapefruit juice
250 ml (1 cup) orange juice

mint sprigs

Place the tea bags in a large heatproof jug and pour in 750 ml (3 cups) boiling water. Allow to steep for 3 minutes, then remove and discard the bags. Stir in the honey and allow to cool.

Add the grapefruit and orange juice. Cover and chill in the refrigerator. Serve in glasses, garnished with mint.

Makes 6 x 250 ml glasses

Mint julep

20 g (1 cup) mint leaves
1 tablespoon sugar
1 tablespoon lemon juice
250 ml (1 cup) pineapple juice
250 ml (1 cup) ginger ale
ice cubes

mint leaves

Roughly chop the mint leaves and place in a heatproof jug with the sugar. Using a wooden spoon, bruise the mint. Add the lemon juice, pineapple juice and 125 ml ($\frac{1}{2}$ cup) boiling water. Mix well. Cover with plastic wrap and leave for 30 minutes.

Strain, then refrigerate until cold.

Just before serving, add the ginger ale and mix well. Serve in glasses over ice and garnish with mint leaves.

Makes 2 x 300 ml glasses

Breakfast shake

150 g fruit (passionfruit, mango,
banana, peaches, strawberries,
blueberries)
250 ml (1 cup) milk
2 teaspoons wheat germ
1 tablespoon honey
60 g (¼ cup) vanilla yoghurt
1 egg, optional
1 tablespoon malt powder

Blend all the ingredients in a blender
for 30–60 seconds, or until well
combined.

Pour into chilled glasses and serve
immediately.

Makes 2 x 325 ml glasses

American iced tea

4 Ceylon tea bags
2 tablespoons sugar
2 tablespoons lemon juice
375 ml (1 ½ cups) dark grape juice
500 ml (2 cups) orange juice
375 ml (1 ½ cups) ginger ale
ice cubes

lemon slices

Place the tea bags in a heatproof bowl with 1 litre boiling water. Leave for 3 minutes. Remove the bags and stir in the sugar. Cool.

Stir in the juices. Refrigerate until cold, then add the ginger ale. Serve over ice cubes with a slice of lemon.

Makes 8 x 250 ml glasses

Cinnamon and custard shake

375 ml (1½ cups) milk
185 ml (¾ cup) prepared custard
3 teaspoons honey
1½ teaspoons ground cinnamon
3 scoops vanilla ice cream

ground cinnamon

Blend together the milk, custard, honey, cinnamon and ice cream until smooth and fluffy.

Pour the shake into tall glasses, sprinkle with the extra cinnamon and serve immediately.

Makes 2 x 375 ml glasses

Choc cherry smoothie

500 ml (2 cups) milk
55 g (¼ cup) whole red glacé cherries
25 g (¼ cup) desiccated coconut
1 tablespoon chocolate topping
3 scoops chocolate ice cream

Blend together the milk, cherries, coconut, topping and ice cream until smooth and fluffy.

Pour into tall glasses and serve immediately.

Makes 2 x 375 ml glasses

Index

INDEX

INDEX

INDEX

Photographers: Jon Bader, Craig Cranko, Joe Filshie, Scott Hawkins, Ian Hofstetter, Andre Martin, Rob Reichenfeld, Brett Stevens, Jon Paul Urizar

Food stylist: Anna-Marie Bruechert, Marie-Hélène Clauzon, Jane Collins, Sarah de Nardi, Georgina Dolling, Carolyn Fienberg, Cherise Koch, Michelle Norianto, Sarah O'Brien, Sally Parker, Maria Villegas

Food preparation: Alison Adams, Valli Little, Tracey Meharg, Kerrie Mullins, Briget Palmer, Kim Passenger, Justine Poole, Christine Sheppard, Angela Tregonning

Special thanks to Wheel & Barrow, Sydney, who supplied props and accessories for the cover and chapter openers.

Published by Murdoch Books® a division of Murdoch Magazines Pty Ltd,
GPO Box 1203, Sydney NSW 2001

Editorial Director: Diana Hill Editor: Katharine Gasparini
Creative Director: Marylouise Brammer Designer: Wing Ping Tong
Food Director: Lulu Grimes
Photographer (chapter openers): Ian Hofstetter Stylist (chapter openers): Cherise Koch
Picture Librarian: Mary Ferizis

Chief Executive: Juliet Rogers
Publisher: Kay Scarlett
Production: Janis Barbi

National Library of Australia Cataloguing-in-Publication Data: Cool Food. Includes index.
ISBN 174045 189 9. 1. Cookery 2. Quick and easy cookery.
641.563

Printed by Sing Cheong Printing Co. Ltd
PRINTED IN HONG KONG

You may find cooking times vary depending on the oven you are using. For fan-forced ovens,
as a general rule, set the oven temperature to 20°C lower than indicated in the recipe.
We have used 20 ml tablespoon measures. If you are using a 15 ml tablespoon, for most recipes
the difference will not be noticeable. However, for recipes using small amounts of flour and cornflour,
add an extra teaspoon for each tablespoon specified. We have used 60 g (Grade 3) eggs in all recipes.

IMPORTANT: Those who might be at risk from the effects of salmonella poisoning (the elderly, pregnant
women, young children and those suffering from immune deficiency diseases) should consult their GP
with any concerns about eating raw eggs.

Published by:
AUSTRALIA
Murdoch Books®Australia
GPO Box 1203
Sydney NSW 2001
Phone: +61 (0) 2 4352 7000
Fax: +61 (0) 2 4352 7026

UK
Murdoch Books® UK
Ferry House
51–57 Lacy Road
London SW15 1PR
Phone: +44 (0) 20 8355 1480
Fax: +44 (0) 20 8355 1499